M. F. S.

Stories of holy lives

M. F. S.

Stories of holy lives

ISBN/EAN: 9783741190520

Manufactured in Europe, USA, Canada, Australia, Japa

Cover: Foto ©Lupo / pixelio.de

Manufactured and distributed by brebook publishing software (www.brebook.com)

M. F. S.

Stories of holy lives

STORIES OF HOLY LIVES.

STORIES OF HOLY LIVES.

By M. F. S.

AUTHOR OF
"STORIES OF THE SAINTS," "CATHERINE HAMILTON," "CATHERINE GROWN OLDER," "TOM'S CRUCIFIX, AND OTHER TALES," ETC.

London:
R. WASHBOURNE, 18 PATERNOSTER ROW.
1875.

Dedicated

TO THE

SACRED HEART OF JESUS,

THE FOUNT AND THE CROWN OF HOLINESS.

CONTENTS.

	PAGE
BLESSED MARGARET MARY	9
BLESSED HENRY SUSO	26
BLESSED PETER FAVRE	37
BLESSED COLOMBINI	52
BLESSED SEBASTIAN VALFRÉ	67
BLESSED IMELDA	81
BLESSED JOHN BERCHMANS	89
BLESSED BENEDICT JOSEPH LABRÈ	111
LOUISA DE CARVAJAL	128

Contents.

	PAGE
CLAUDE AND MARIE DE LA GARAYE	147
MADAME DE MIRAMION	158
VEN. ANNA MARIA TAIGI	177
ANNE CATHERINE EMMERICH	192
CURÉ D'ARS	211
MARIE EUSTELLE HARPAIN	232
M. OLIER	251

STORIES OF HOLY LIVES.

Blessed Margaret Mary.

UPON the feast of S. Mary Magdalen, the 22nd July, 1647, a little child came into the world whose soul had been chosen to understand and teach to men the secret of the burning love contained in the Sacred Heart of our Divine Lord. Claude and Philiberte Alacoque, the parents of this infant, were pious and devout people, who sought above all things to train their little family for God; and as Margaret was their only girl, the good mother tried especially to lead her to the love of everything which was pure and holy, so that she might in a faint measure resemble Mary, the Mother of God, the type and model of all that is beautiful in the character of either girl or woman. The little child amply rewarded all the care bestowed on her, for she seemed in her earliest infancy to learn the love and fear of God. At three years of age it was sufficient to say to her "You are going to offend God," as a check upon any childish fault which seemed bursting forth. When she was but four years old she would run to church alone, and kneel there with clasped hands in perfect silent happiness; and when they found her thus, perhaps hours after, and asked what she had been doing, she would answer, "I was thinking of things I have been taught, and I feel as if my heart loves Jesus in the Tabernacle so much." The little girl loved to go to Mass, although not old enough to thoroughly understand the mysteries of the Holy Sacrifice, and she seemed quite content to kneel there adoring Jesus, never complaining of the cold, however great, though it was often severely felt by many an older person.

Her mother's lessons of the virtues of Mary made a great impression upon the little Margaret. She dreamed over the events of the sweet life of that blessed heavenly mother, and in simple words offered her many a prayer, and told her every little difficulty or trouble. Later, she vowed to fast on Saturdays, and as soon as she could read she would recite the Office of the Immaculate Conception, and when she said the rosary, if she was alone she would lie prostrate, kissing the ground at every Ave Maria. Margaret was always asking every one to teach her how to pray. In her simplicity she did not know that every act of love to Jesus in the Tabernacle was in itself a prayer; and at last, as no one gave her the instruction she wanted, she begged God to help her to understand how to make her prayer to Him. In answer to this entreaty, it seemed taught her from heaven to kneel humbly before her Lord, adoring

His majesty, and asking of Him the pardon of her sins, and then telling Him every hope or desire of her heart. From this she seemed led on by the Holy Spirit to meditate on the mysteries and actions of Christ's human life, finding there lessons of humility and charity, which she tried to practise in her own path of daily duty. All this was at an age when many children have no other thought than their pleasure and play. Margaret seemed to have but one word ever filling her with eager desire, and that word was "prayer."

At nine years of age this little girl had the joy of making her First Communion under the instruction of some nuns of the Order of S. Clare, with whom, after the death of her father, Margaret had been placed. The child's disposition was naturally lively, affectionate, and easily impressed, and Jesus, longing to make this loving little heart entirely His own, gave her thus early this great grace. After that First Communion, it seemed that her Lord would not let her love anything but

Himself, reproaching her for every little unfaithfulness, and turning all earthly pleasure into bitterness, so that she could not rest in it. Then she was laid for four years upon her bed, without power to move or walk or help herself. The illness was long and wearisome, and nothing appeared to benefit her until the child thought of making herself by vow the special care of the Blessed Virgin, and her recovery was immediate. From that day Margaret made Mary the mistress of her heart, and was taught by her to know and do God's Will, and to correct her faults. One day, when she was sitting down while saying the Rosary, her heavenly Mother appeared before her and said, "I am surprised, my child, that you serve me so carelessly;" and though she was very young, Margaret never forgot that reproof, and redoubled her efforts to be earnest and reverent in every prayer and devotion. At thirteen years old she was giving two hours in the early morning and two hours at night to prayer, and Jesus in the Blessed Sacrament attracted her with such sweet force, that she did not know how to quit His presence.

One thought, one desire occupied her then—the longing to be consumed by love as she knelt before Him, even as the waxen lights burned down and died away, having done no other service than offer their little tribute of homage at His feet.

Still at an age when children are not usually called by God to practise mortification in any special way, it was remarkable that Margaret Alacoque was regularly fasting three times a week, and using instruments of penance to punish her body and keep it in subjection. Besides leading her to these exercises, God saw fit to send her other trials and sufferings far more difficult to receive and bear with meekness and joy. The affairs of Margaret's mother were then very much embarrassed, and they often needed both food and clothing. In their own home they were held in a sort of captivity by those who, pretending to assist, ruled over the family with cruel tyranny, not

Blessed Margaret Mary. 15

even being free to go to church without permission, and yet Margaret never murmured or repined. During this time she was so fearful of doing anything against charity, that she would not even talk over their wrongs with her mother. Whenever her thoughts turned upon these sufferings, she checked them by remembering that all things came from God, and, however hard, were meant as a means of purifying her soul.

Jesus saw all her difficulties, and saw too her patience, and as a help in bearing her hard life, He gave her such a love of the Cross that all its pain seemed gone, and she desired only to suffer that she might be more truly His servant. Although she had tasted so much of God's love and goodness, Margaret was to find a great difficulty in giving herself to her Divine Spouse in holy religion—a strong temptation came upon her to love prayer less and take time from it to give to the world. She would increase her austerities, hoping to find peace from the reproaches of her conscience. She would pray God to show her the way in which she could most perfectly please Him, and yet feel afraid lest her prayer should be answered, and she be led to embrace the life which suddenly seemed so hard.

All this was perhaps permitted to render her sacrifice more acceptable to God, for one day in prayer her eyes were opened to see the beauty of holiness under the vows of religion; and bursting into tears of sorrow for her unfaithfulness and resistance to grace, she promised herself to God in whatever way He should show her to be His Divine Will.

Upon the 25th of May, 1671, when she was twenty-two years of age, Margaret entered the convent of the Visitation in Paray-le-Monial. God still guided her soul, but it was by teaching her to receive His communications through her superiors. Finding out her love of penance, the mistress of novices would refuse her the mortifications she desired, giving instead others so disagreeable to her natural feelings, that it required all her courage and all her faith to yield with obedience. At such times she would call God to assist her, and her cry was not in vain. However hard or however unsuitable seemed the commands laid upon her, she received grace to execute them faithfully, and to find in them health of soul.

Our Lord loved His servant so much that He would not pass over the slightest offence she committed against Him without reproaching her. For a slight movement of vanity, a word contrary to simplicity, He made her so to understand His sorrow, that her tears flowed fast, and she would beg His forgiveness with the greatest anguish of heart. Above all it was given her to understand the pain our Lord experiences from the want of reverence shown to the Most Holy Sacrament, even by nuns in their time of prayer and office. A small distraction, a wandering look, a careless posture, which to so many would seem matters of indifference, Margaret saw to be so many ways of grieving Jesus. For any such fault which she herself committed she would at once go and ask to be given a penance, because many times her Divine Master had told her that any little punishment accepted by obedience was more satisfaction than a great austerity taken up by her own will.

With such a Master, so often speaking to her, so constantly guiding her, the blessed Margaret Mary could not fail to grow daily in virtue and holiness. There were times when, in thinking of the favours He poured upon her, she felt so unworthy to receive them, that she even asked Him to visit souls less unfaithful, souls which should profit more by such great grace. But Jesus had chosen her not for her worthiness, but for her love, and her humility only served to unite Him more closely with her. Margaret Mary had a constant, intense longing for Holy Communion: it was like the "hungering and thirsting after justice" of which our Saviour speaks in His Sermon on the Mount; far stronger, far more irresistible than hunger or thirst of body; and after having received Jesus into her heart, she would kneel as one wholly lost in love and adoration, filled with a great peace, in which she listened to the voice of Him who had visited her. All the night before receiving the Blessed Sacrament she could think of nothing but the happiness which the morning would bring: even in her dreams she was speaking with Him as if in prayer. It was in the Holy Communion that Jesus communicated special graces. One day He showed her the treatment His sacred Body received from one who approached the Sacrament in sin. She saw Him torn and trampled on, lying at the feet of the one who thus outraged Him, and a voice said, "See how sinners treat me."

But the most wonderful revelation granted to this humble religious was that of the devotion which Jesus desired to see offered to His Sacred Heart, and the thought was so new and strange, that Margaret Mary had to pass through many discouragements and difficulties in making it known. One day, when kneeling before the Blessed Sacrament exposed on the altar, she felt strongly penetrated with a sense of God's presence, and in a clear form Jesus appeared before her, pointing to His Heart, which concealed within it such treasures of love for men. Having spoken to her of the infinite charity which He had for all creatures, and especially towards herself, a charity which was so little known, the Divine Vision asked her for the gift of her own heart as the price of what He was about to bestow. Gladly she offered Him what He sought, and then it seemed to her that her Lord took her heart, placing it within His own, where it appeared like a little atom lost in an ardent furnace, the furnace of the Saviour's love. What a joy, what a grace, to see in vision her heart resting within that of her Spouse, to hear Him say, "From this time you shall be called the disciple of the Sacred Heart;" to know her work should be to make known to others the burning fire of charity with which our Lord is filled! No wonder that Margaret Mary

Alacoque talked ever of the wonders she had seen, of the desire with which Jesus waited to know that the treasures of that Sacred Heart were understood.

It must have cost her much to see her superior's doubtful, cold suspicions, thinking her to be under some great delusion. It must have been hard to bear the many trials of humility and obedience with which she was proved, but through it all she heard in spirit the sweet voice of the Tabernacle whispering, "Learn of me, for I am meek and lowly of heart;" and so she waited and prayed on in faith and love.

This servant of God suffered much in mind and body for the sake of others; she used to pray that God would accept her as a victim for some of the sins which were daily committed against Him, and He was pleased to grant her request. It was at the carnival time—the time just before Lent, when there was formerly so much sinful amusement and boisterous mirth—that Margaret Mary suffered most severely, feeling in mind some of the agony which Jesus experienced when His own people mocked at His thorn-crowned head, and in body bearing great pains which reduced her to a state of helpless weakness. Each carnival time she was like one dying, but as a proof that her sufferings were supernatural, God always raised her up on Ash Wednesday in health and strength to bear the Lenten fast.

In her life as a nun she filled many different offices. She was employed to help in the infirmary, then to take charge of the children educated there, whom she tried to train in the love of God and His dear Mother; but perhaps it was as mistress of novices that Sister Margaret Mary seemed to receive especial grace and benediction from heaven. In her lessons to those under her care she never lost an opportunity of seeking to inspire them with the devotion to the Sacred Heart which filled her own soul; and one of the happiest days of her life was when at length these novices were inspired to pay that homage to their Divine Spouse which their good mother had prayed and longed to see.

It was upon her feast day, in the year 1685, that in their love and respect for her, these young people ornamented a little altar with flowers, and placed it in the novitiate, with a picture upon it of the Heart of Jesus surrounded with flames, before which they offered their prayers during the day. Sister Margaret Mary prostrated herself before this image and symbol of the ardent charity of Christ, and consecrated herself to that Sacred Heart with such a power of earnest desire, that her novices were inflamed with the same love, and one by one pronounced aloud the same act of consecration.

Never had feast day been so joyous and so holy to the good nun. She saw then how God would bring about those designs in which He had chosen to use her as an instrument, and fresh hope and confidence filled her heart. But the doings of the novices were not approved by the community, and there was more discouragement and disbelief to be gone through; but at length the devotion which has now spread through all the Catholic Church was taken up by the religious of the convent where Margaret Mary had prayed and suffered, and then her happiness was intense. Many a vision was granted her, in which Jesus taught her more particularly the method of honouring His Sacred Heart; and when the devotion had taken root, and bid fair to grow deep and strong as time passed by, her work was ended. Death was to her the way of being united with her Lord for ever, and in it there was no dread. Her joy as she thought of leaving the world was edifying to all the sisters in the convent, and yet it was still more beautiful to see her perfect willingness to live and bear the cross, if by so doing she could better fulfil the Divine purpose. After receiving the last sacraments, and placing herself anew within the Sacred Heart of Jesus, she died upon the 17th of October, 1690, at the age of forty-two years.

"O Lord Jesus Christ, who in wonderful revelations didst manifest to the Blessed Margaret Mary the incomprehensible riches of Thy Heart, grant that by her merits and example we may love Thee in all things, and above all things, and become worthy to receive a place in Thy adorable Heart for ever. Amen."

Blessed Henry Suso.

AT Neberlingen, near Constance, on the festival of S. Benedict, in the year 1300, Henry Suso was born of a good and noble family. His mother was a person of such great holiness, that her son venerated her next to the Blessed Virgin and the Saints of God; and it was in his devotion that, instead of using the surname of his father, he took her maiden name of "Seuss," which he latinised into Suso, and bore ever after. At thirteen years of age Henry Suso entered into the novitiate of the Dominicans, who had a foundation in Constance, and in due time he was allowed to take religious vows there, thus gaining the desire which had been in his heart from the earliest days of childhood.

After some years, in which he made steady progress in the love and service of Almighty God, he was sent to the Dominicans at Cologne, so that he might pursue those studies which were necessary to fit him for doing good to the souls of men, and there he was soon promoted to the degree of a "doctor of theology." Many would have been pleased with their success, but in the heart of Henry Suso a Divine voice seemed speaking clearly and strongly, forbidding him to accept this honour, and he could not but obey its warnings. All God's servants can only be safe by following closely His inspirations, and as in some cases He causes them to know that learning and honour, and even high position, are His gifts, and must be accepted and used for His glory, so to others, as to blessed Henry Suso, He makes known His Will, that they should pass through life by a more hidden path, in which they can best do a work in the souls of others. Thus this holy Dominican friar gave himself up to preach with great earnestness, and he had the happiness of converting many sinners, and leading souls that already loved God to a better way of following Him. His own soul was one of those chosen out for those strange, close communications with the Almighty which we cannot wholly understand. He was penetrated with such a sense of his sinfulness and unworthiness, that his constant acts of contrition and humility drew God down to him in wonderful union, so that in his time of prayer his whole heart seemed poured out and lost in Divine love, in which he heard a heavenly voice instructing and guiding him in holy things. Once, in a moment of fervour, he pierced the flesh just above his heart, and imprinted there the Holy Name, caring nothing for the pain of the wound or the blood which flowed from it; then kneeling down, he besought Jesus to imprint His dear Name so deeply within his heart, that it might never for a moment be forgotten. After a while the wound healed up, but the letters of the Name remained always plainly upon his flesh, and if he gazed on it in any trouble which befell him, that trouble seemed directly lightened of its weight. When the Blessed Henry was called by the bell to his meals, he used to kneel for a moment, asking his Divine Lord to go with him to table, and he would try to picture Jesus in the place opposite, and thus eat and drink with the remembrance of His presence. He had a great liking for fruit, but, inspired by God, he refrained from eating it until his taste was completely subdued, when, in obedience to the Divine Will made known to him, he again partook of it in company with others. It seemed as if Jesus was always so visibly present to his mind, that he was as one who walked in body by our Lord's side in even the smallest action of his daily life. Sleeping, rising, eating, preaching, or praying, his heart was wholly turned to his Divine Master, and to the most perfect way of imitating Him.

His penances were severe, but they were all done for the pure motive of accomplishing

God's Will. The scourge, the hair-shirt, the fast or vigil, were all well known to him in his work of killing nature, that so his spirit might truly live; but all these helps would have done nothing in making him holy but for the spirit in which he executed them and the obedience with which they were taken up or laid aside without self-pleasing.

According to his Dominican rule, the Blessed Henry had frequently to undertake long journeys, during which he was preaching and teaching in the Name of God; and many difficulties and sicknesses befel him, but he always turned with full confidence to the thought of God's unfailing protection, and found comfort thus.

In many towns people turned against him, and spread evil reports of his character. In one place there was a monastery which possessed a large stone crucifix of the size, it was said, of Christ Himself. Upon a day in Lent fresh blood was observed upon the crucifix, beneath the wound on the left side, and when

Blessed Henry, like other people, went to gaze with wonder, he drew close and received the blood upon his finger in the sight of all. The throng became greater, and as they pressed round the holy man they forced him to tell what he had seen and done; and he did so, only declaring that he dared not pronounce any opinion whether this strange thing was the work of God or man. The story was passed about from lip to lip, and changing and growing as such stories do, there were those who did not hesitate to say that Blessed Henry had drawn blood from his own finger and rubbed it on the crucifix, in order to deceive the people and make them suppose the crucifix was miraculous. The people of that part soon became so angry and enraged, that he had to escape by night in great haste, or they would have fallen on him to kill him; and gladly as Henry Suso would have given up life for Christ, he knew God called him then to save himself, and continue in his work of teaching men.

Another time, during a journey, the blessed

man fell into a great stream of water, having upon him a little book he had just finished writing, which he hoped God would make useful to many souls. He was being swept away by the strong current, when by the Divine Providence there came up a young man, who ventured into the stream and saved the life of God's servant.

Again, on another journey during very cold weather, he had travelled a whole day without tasting food, when he came to a deep, rapid piece of water, and the man who drove the carriage in which the Blessed Henry was seated went carelessly too near the bank, so that the holy man fell into the stream. He could not turn on either side, because the carriage had fallen over him, and in this state he was floated some distance down towards a mill. Several persons ran to help draw him out, but it was not for some time, and with great difficulty, that they succeeded in bringing him to land, dripping wet and almost exhausted. His teeth chattered with cold, and there was no village or town near, wherein he could be warmed or refreshed, and in this miserable state he called upon God to aid him. At last, on the hill, he espied a very small village, and there, all frozen and wet, he made his way, which took him so long, that night had set in when he reached the door. In God's name he begged for shelter, but was driven away from house after house. No one pitied him, no one cared for his misery, and then the cold and fatigue seemed to attack his heart, so that he feared for his life, and cried aloud to God to befriend him. These words of prayer were overheard by a peasant who had already, like the rest, driven the holy man from his door, but now Divine Grace changed his heart, and, repenting of his unkindness, he raised the sufferer in his arms and gave him shelter until morning.

Many as were the troubles which God permitted to overtake Blessed Henry Suso one after another, it happened sometimes that a time of peace and rest was granted him, but this was never a cause of joy; loving suffering for the sake of being conformed to the likeness of his Master, he felt that things were going very ill with him when no one attacked his good name or treated him unkindly, and it seemed as if God had forgotten him, until fresh trials were granted. Many persons were drawn to begin a spiritual life by his earnest teaching and holy example; many put far from them all earthly love for the love of God; and when, after many years of constant labour and suffering, the blessed man died, he was missed and mourned by all his spiritual children. It was on the Feast of the Conversion of S. Paul, in the year 1865, that he passed from this world, while he was staying in the city of Ulm, and he was buried in the cloister of the Dominican convent there.

Two hundred years went by,—years which had seen his name almost forgotten,—when some workmen, digging the foundations for a new building, came by accident upon the body of Blessed Henry Suso, lying clothed in the Dominican habit, still incorrupt, and sending forth a most sweet fragrance. The men went in fear and surprise to the burgomaster of that city, but he bade them fill up the grave and keep the matter secret. However, it was not God's Will that the sanctity of His servant should remain hidden, and many devout persons went to the spot and obtained morsels of his habit, which have been since distributed and prized amongst Catholics. At a later period efforts were made to discover the sacred remains, but without success; but his name has not died from out of the hearts of men, and his feast is kept on the 2nd of March by the Dominican order, with the approbation of Pope Gregory XVI.

"When a man has died to self, and begun to live in Christ, it is well with him," was one of the spiritual maxims of Blessed Henry Suso, and one which contains the secret of his great holiness. It was the daily unflinching warfare against self, the crucifixion of his natural tastes and desires, which made his heart ready for the rich graces God bestowed upon him, and drew him onward to a life "hidden with Christ in God." Nor was this left for the work of his manhood, for Henry Suso took upon himself early the sweet yoke of Christ, and fought bravely against the temptations of childhood and youth, and thus he—like his Master when upon earth—grew in God's favour with each advancing year, until his warfare was ended, his work done, and his soul rested in the fulness of everlasting bliss.

Blessed Peter Favre.

IN the little village of Villaret, amidst the mountains of Savoy, there is still shown a stone upon which a boy of six or seven years would stand, talking to the children who gathered round him about God and holy things. This boy was Peter Favre, who became so great and zealous a preacher in after years.

He was born there in 1506, during the Easter festival time, and his parents, if poor in worldly goods, were rich in piety and true Christian virtue, whose great desire was to train Peter in the service of God. From the earliest age it seemed as if the child's soul was specially enlightened by the Holy Spirit, so that he was much drawn to prayer and loving thoughts of God; and though at all times his food was scanty and coarse, he denied himself in many things, that he might learn mortification early. His daily task about this time was to take care of a small flock of sheep, but he loved to hear Mass so much, that he tried to think of a plan by which he could go to the church without any harm coming to the sheep. There is a little spring of very clear water near Villaret which still bears the name of "Blessed Peter Favre's fountain," and it is said that, having no means of giving water to the sheep, he prayed to God, and the spring gushed forth by a miracle out of the rock; and every morning when the church clock struck six the little boy collected his flock all round this fountain, and ran off to Mass, in perfect confidence that he should find them safe upon his return, and he was right—never did one stray away from the little spring during the time he was assisting at the Holy Sacrifice.

God often shows in very early years the special work to which He calls souls which are wholly given to Him, and thus in Peter Favre it was seen how strongly he was attracted as a child to teach others the catechism, the prayers, and the holy lessons which his good mother had instructed him in.

Many other girls and boys were also keeping sheep upon the mountains, and these he would gather round him, preaching them little sermons, which he ended by reciting the rosary. So simply and sweetly did the child speak of God, that even older persons loved to listen to him, and when he finished they would give him pence, or apples and walnuts and other fruits. The money Peter always took to his mother, the fruit he would share amongst the poorest little boys he knew.

As the child grew older he began to beg very earnestly that his father and mother would send him to school, and they would gladly have done so, but, being poor, it was a difficult matter to find means of granting his desire. At last an opportunity was found of sending him to a priest in a little town two leagues distant from Villaret, and thus Peter began to read and write, progressing so rapidly, that in two years he was well advanced as a Latin scholar.

Having done so much, his parents resolved to let him follow the studies he loved, and he was placed at the college of La Roche, under the care of a very learned man, who was also holy and well fitted to guide the lads who lived with him. This good master proved a great help to Favre, and the boy soon distanced his companions in learning, and also in piety, for his whole heart was turned to prayer when school hours were over, and every spare moment was spent either in this exercise or in the reading of spiritual books.

We hear that Peter had a frank, pleasant manner, which made him a general favourite, and his innocent face reflected the simplicity and purity of his heart. At about twelve years of age he longed to have some gift to present to God, and when he prayed he used to ask to be guided in an offering which would be pleasing to the Almighty. During the holiday-time, when he was at home with his parents, he went one day into a lonely place some distance from the village, and there he knelt down, and lifting up his heart to God, made this request for light to know His Will, which he had often made before. It seemed that nothing could be too great, nothing half great enough to give to One whose favours had been poured out upon him ever since his birth, and he longed with an intense desire to offer his life to God. The boy's earnest love drew down upon him fresh proofs of the Divine favour, and an inward voice seemed to tell him that God would be well pleased with the offering of a vow of constant purity; and in a moment he made it, promising to regard himself as consecrated for ever to the service of his Creator. From that time his progress in heavenly things was still more remarkable, and God's blessing also rested upon his studies, so that he advanced rapidly in all that he undertook, until his master thought it needful for him to receive more instruction than he himself could give. It was thus that Peter Favre was led to Paris, where he was afterwards to meet the great S. Ignatius, whose influence upon his soul should produce so much fruit. It was in September, 1525, that the youth of nineteen years left his home and early friends to enter the college of S. Barbara in the great French city, where for a companion he had Francis Xavier; and in the year 1529 Ignatius of Loyola joined the students there, and became the friend of Peter Favre. Just then Peter was in a very unhappy state of mind. Though his desires were so pure, God, as a trial, permitted the evil spirit to whisper dreadful temptations to him. He was also tormented by feelings of gluttony, and although in all this he did not sin, because he was hating the temptations and fighting against them constantly, his heart was cast down with the fear of giving way and grieving God.

All this misery was hidden in Peter's own heart until the load became more than he could endure; and one day, by chance as it seemed, though really it was the inspiration of God's Holy Spirit, he told his friend Ignatius a great part of his spiritual troubles.

Nothing could be more unsafe and unwise than to speak of what concerns the soul to people generally, but being done to one like Ignatius of Loyola, who had gone through many temptations and struggles in his first turning to God, it became the means of bringing peace and happiness of heart to Peter Favre, and from that time they had long and delightful conversations about spiritual things. Ignatius received light from God to guide the soul of Favre to great detachment and generous love, and after they had known each other well for two years, he confided to his friend his own hope of going to the Holy Land, when his studies were finished, there to labour to convert the infidels. But although this was the great desire of his heart, Ignatius was not obstinate in attaching his will to it. He declared to Favre that if the scheme was not approved he should offer himself to the Pope, to work wherever it was thought that he could be most useful to the souls of men. Favre was very much impressed with the words of Ignatius, so full of ardour, and yet breathing such true humility and love for God's holy Will, and he promised to go with him wherever he might be sent, and take up the work of a soldier of the Cross. Francis Xavier and three other young men also desired to become fellow-workers with them, and thus a little band of earnest fervent souls were drawn by the love of their Master to devote themselves to a life of toil and sacrifice, such as His had been on earth before.

In the year 1533 Favre had nearly closed his course of study, so he went to Villaret to pay a last visit to the home of his childhood. His mother had died before that time, but he remained some months in the little village with his father, and returned to Paris without a single coin in his possession. On reaching that city, he retired by the wish of S. Ignatius to a poor house, where he could go through the spiritual exercises.

It was winter time then, so severe a winter that the ice upon the river Seine was solid enough to bear the weight of carts. Frozen snow was everywhere, and yet Peter used to pray and meditate by night and by day in an open courtyard, where the keen wind blew upon him sharply. He also, as a penance, fasted so severely, that during the first six days he neither tasted a morsel of bread nor a drop of water; and he would have carried this austerity still further, if S. Ignatius had not commanded him to refresh himself with food, and allow himself a fire. But those forty days in which he gave himself to prayer and self-examination did a great work in the soul of Peter Favre. Many temptations left him, many graces were given him, and when the time was ended he was prepared to receive Holy Orders with great fervour, and on the Feast of S. Mary Magdalene, 1534, he for the first time offered the holy sacrifice of the Mass. Upon the Feast of the Assumption in the same year, Ignatius, with Peter Favre and his other companions, went to the church at Montmartre, to vow themselves solemnly to visit Jerusalem, and then to put themselves under obedience to the sovereign Pontiff, to work for souls according as he judged best; and this vow was renewed in the two following years upon the same day and in the same church by all but Ignatius, who had left Paris for Biscay on account of severe illness. After a year and a half passed without his help and care, these young men started for Venice, where their leader awaited them, passing on foot through Lorraine and Germany, and suffering from the severity of the winter and dangers arising from the war between France and Spain. The journey was accomplished safely at last, and they stayed in Venice, serving the hospitals, until they could go to Rome in Lent, to obtain the blessing of Pope Paul III.

But the way did not seem to open for them to go to Jerusalem, so that the Holy Father gave to Ignatius and his friends the power to teach and preach in any place, and Peter Favre was sent to Parma, where he was engaged in hearing confessions, giving the spiritual exercises, and leading many souls to turn to God. Later he went to Ratisbon where he made his profession, with the usual vows, and the further vow of obedience to the Pope as to the labours to be engaged in, and this act brought fresh peace and strength to his soul. Spain also he visited, being cast into prison on his way there, as he journeyed through France, Portugal, Savoy, and back again to Germany. To him it mattered not to what place he might be sent, there were souls everywhere which would be lost or saved; souls for which the Saviour had died, and for which He would have died again had more suffering and sacrifice been necessary for their redemption, and this thought made Favre toil on so bravely amidst fatigue and difficulty.

The first miracle which God appears to have granted to Father Peter Favre, took place during his stay in Gandia, where his holy life had won for him the loving reverence of the whole city. One day he knelt in prayer before a picture of the Blessed Virgin which hung in the ducal chapel, and it was distinctly seen by all who were there at the time that Our Lady's eyes suddenly appeared to open, turning with a sweet and gentle expression towards her faithful servant. The news soon spread, and the picture was known after by the name of "Our Lady of the Miracle," and later, when it was conveyed to the Carmelite convent at Madrid, many proofs of God's miraculous power were shown there.

But this life of unceasing toil began to affect the health of the Blessed Favre, and after leaving Gandia for Barcelona, a tertian fever attacked him, which reduced him to extreme weakness, and he was still in a very delicate state when he started for Rome.

It was seven years since he had been seen

there, and the Fathers of the Society were rejoiced to have him with them once more, but they were soon alarmed by a fresh attack of illness, in which remedies seemed of no avail.

Favre himself was calm and happy, longing to be for ever with God, and yet willing to live and work on, if such work was for His greater glory.

While his friends wept bitterly as they thought of his death, the holy man bade them rather give thanks on his behalf to God, who not only was so good as to take him from the world, but who also had granted his great desire to die in the arms of his father, S. Ignatius. Upon the first of August he received the last Sacraments, and then, fixing every thought on his Saviour in humble love and perfect trust, he died very quietly in the presence of many of his brothers, and of his friend and father, Ignatius, who had been the means, under God, of leading him into the path of holiness which he had pursued with so much courage and so much love.

Every one who had known Peter Favre mourned greatly for his loss, and felt persuaded that he was admitted into the company of the saints in heaven, and a great devotion to his memory spread throughout Savoy and his native village.

Sixteen years after his death, the room where he was born was turned into a little chapel, which in later times was rebuilt and beautified; and here persons of all ranks have knelt in prayer, asking for many favours through his intercession, and asking, as we may believe, some of that generous love for God which carried blessed Peter Favre through the contest against temptation and trial and every difficulty, and brought him safely to heaven at last.

"May our Lord grant to me and to every one these two feet, true fear and true love; for with them we must mount the ladder of the way of God." Such were his own words, some of those words which have been preserved for the help and comfort of many souls; and, like him, we also by these means —fear of self and of sin, and love of God and of our neighbour for His sake—shall gain the same rest and the same reward. And though the way may be long, and though it may be weary, and the steps upon the ladder which leads to holiness seem hard to take and harder still to keep, the same help which has sustained the saints and servants of God will not be refused us if we seek it by constant, patient prayer.

Blessed Colombini.

AMONG the many holy men and women whose birthplace has been the ancient city of Siena, is Giovanni Colombini, who became one of God's favoured servants. His parents were well-born, and, still better, were devout and pious people, who sought to train their son in the fear and love of the Almighty; but no records of his early years have been made known to us, and it seems that he grew up like many other youths—not one of the enemies of God, seeking indeed to keep His commandments and avoid grievous sin, yet a stranger to that ardent love which was afterwards to effect so great a change in his soul. Arrived at manhood, Giovanni married as befitted his position, and a son and daughter were afterwards born to him; and then it seemed that he grew too much concerned about earthly matters, seeking only success and prosperity in this life, until he was converted by the mercy and grace of God.

It has often happened that some trifling event appears to change the entire life of one whom our Lord chooses for His service. Some word, some book, some circumstance which looks like chance, but really is a part of God's providence, rouses the sleeping soul, and in a moment reveals its danger, and thus it was with Colombini. One day, when he returned home from his business, the dinner was not ready, as usual, and he grew very angry with his wife and his servants, saying that it was necessary he should return at once to attend to his affairs. Though he spoke roughly and impatiently, his wife did not answer him in the same way. She begged him to wait but a very little time, and the meal would be served; and putting before him a book containing the lives and legends of the Saints, she asked him to employ the moments of waiting in reading of those holy ones who were so beloved of God.

But Giovanni got still more angry, and throwing the book across the room, cried, " It is fine for thee to think of legends; as for me, I must return to my warehouse."

But even as he spoke his heart reproached him, so that he felt constrained to pick up the book, and as he sat down to wait, he turned the leaves carelessly, still murmuring at the unwonted delay. Suddenly his eye was fixed upon the page before him, some word attracted him, and he read a few lines of the life of S. Mary of Egypt, the great sinner, but afterwards the true penitent, and almost unconsciously he went on, until his wife returned to say that dinner waited on the table.

But Giovanni's interest was so engaged that he could not lay down the story. As he read, the wonderful love and pity of God melted his heart, and he exclaimed, " *Thou* must wait now, for I shall finish this legend." His wife was glad to see the book had pleased him, it was not the custom of Giovanni to read good books, and many a time she had prayed that a change might pass over him; and now it seemed that her desire was granted, for that history made so deep an impression on his soul, that he thought of little else by day or night. With his mind turned so much to this story of contrition, Giovanni could not be so anxious about worldly gains as he had been; and beginning to see how sinfully he had grudged alms and prevented his family from doing anything to help others, he resolved to punish himself by giving more than was asked of him, and also by paying more money than was due to those who sold him anything. God, who looked down with approval upon this struggle against the passion of avarice, gave him more grace, so that he next began to fast and to pray; and thus he advanced every day in the ways of holiness, until his heart burned with so great a love of Jesus that he longed to give up all he had, like the disciples of old, to follow Him.

So Giovanni Colombini, who had once been well clad, began to dress meanly, and allow himself to be despised by others. He also practised many hard penances, sleeping sometimes on a bench during the whole night, excepting the hours which he gave to prayer. At this time Giovanni met one day with one of his former friends, a man highly esteemed in the city, to whom he talked so earnestly of the happiness of following Christ in poverty and humiliation, that Francesco was touched with a desire to do the same, and they both began to give away amongst the poor the money which they had taken such pains to heap up. The wife of this holy man had often wished in the days of his worldliness that Giovanni might be converted to God. She was also a well-disposed and religious woman, and yet when she witnessed all this benevolence to the poor, she became angry, and reproached her husband with wasting the money which was her right. He would gently answer her that she should rather thank God, who had heard her prayers; but this vexed her still more, and she cried, "I prayed for rain, but I did not pray for a deluge." Like so many of us, she had hoped to be answered as *she* thought well, and did not feel willing that God should do it in His own way. Then Giovanni would speak to her of the vanity of human riches, and reminding her that the treasures laid up in heaven would alone avail when death should come, he strove to calm her anger, but with little success, until God vouchsafed to work a miracle, which reconciled her to her husband's good works. It happened one day that Giovanni and his friend Francesco were going to hear Mass, when they saw at the church door a poor man sick with leprosy. Seeing his misery, these two holy servants of God were moved with compassion, and for the love of Christ they overcame their natural repugnance, and, raising him from the ground, carried him carefully to the house of Giovanni. His wife was disgusted at the horrible appearance of the leper, and cried, "Are these the goods thou bringest me? I will leave my house, and then thou canst do as thou pleasest, as it is thy custom to do."

Giovanni gently besought her to be merciful to the sufferer, saying that any service rendered to him was rendered to Christ, but all was in vain; and finding that she would not yield to his persuasions, Giovanni began to prepare a warm bath, in which he washed the leper, and then, laying him in the best bed the house contained, returned to church to hear Mass, begging his wife to visit the sufferer during his absence.

The lady was very angry, and would not promise to do this, but her conscience became so uneasy that at length she rose up and went to the room where the leprous beggar was lying. As she opened the door a most sweet fragrance came from the bed, so sweet, that Mona drew back through fear, as she remembered the bitter words she had spoken to her husband, and as she stood outside, Giovanni returned from church. "Why dost thou weep?" he asked, upon which Mona began to relate what had happened, and how she durst not enter the room from which such heavenly fragrance issued. So Giovanni and his friend Francesco went in, and, hastening to the bed, uncovered it. Ah! there was no one there : it had been Jesus Himself Who had taken that leprous form, and thus proved the love and devotion of His servants. Then the lady wept more bitterly at the thought that she had complained so angrily at receiving One Who was her Lord and King, and she cried, "Give what thou wilt to God, I will oppose thee in no way." So Giovanni gave thanks to the Almighty, who had thus overcome the resistance of his wife, and he began to seek advice as to how better to devote himself to the service of God.

Many holy and devout men were dwelling in Siena at that time, and all whom Giovanni spoke to, agreed in telling him that the surest and nearest way of following Christ was by the practice of great poverty. So the two friends, after much prayer, resolved to give up home and all they loved, so that they might more closely tread in the footprints of their Master. The only son of Colombini had died a short time before this, so he had but his daughter to provide for; and having placed her in a convent of the Benedictine order, he divided all his possessions between two religious houses, on condition that they should supply his wife every year with sufficient income to live with comfort. Everything now was given to God, and the holy man, accompanied by his friend Francesco (who had also divested himself of all his goods), began asking alms, and for the love of Christ suffered hunger and thirst, reproach and contempt, wearing only scanty robes, and those often patched, while with bare head and feet they did the work of servants at the palace where once they had been esteemed. They carried water, swept the halls, cleaned the kitchens, and accepted the most degrading employment, all in reparation for the pride they had once felt in being well esteemed in the city. For two years these men practised a life of severe penance, and every one ridiculed them, but at length their example began to attract others who longed to serve Christ more perfectly, and some of these joined Colombini and Francesco in their poverty, and went about preaching the love and mercy of Christ, turning many sinners to repentance.

Among the wonderful conversions which took place, there was one, the case of a rich young nobleman of Siena, who was wholly given up to worldly pleasure. Giovanni had often longed to win this youth to the service of his Master, and one day, when Tommaso had followed him in sport, the holy man was inspired to speak to him. They had reached a point where three roads met, and a great wooden cross was placed there; so, guided by God, Giovanni, turning, said, "Tommaso, wilt thou, for the love of Christ, do me a favour?" The young man answered that he would gladly assist him. Then said Giovanni, "I pray thee kneel down at the foot of that cross, and for the love of Jesus say one Pater noster and Ave." Tommaso answered, "If that is the favour thou dost ask, I will readily grant it;" and so, uncovering his head, he knelt, and began the Pater noster, and meanwhile Giovanni knelt too, praying earnestly to God for the conversion of this young man. After a few seconds Tommaso threw himself at the feet of the holy man. God had mercifully enlightened his heart, and shown the misery of sin and the beauty of holiness, and all he desired was to be one of those few followers of Christ, sharing their poverty and humiliation.

Giovanni could not refuse, and so the once worldly Tommaso cast off his rich attire, and dressing meanly like the rest, gave himself up to a life of penance, and faithfully persevered in it, to the great surprise of the people of that city.

Not content with the hardships he daily suffered, Giovanni was always mourning over the time when he had been wholly bent upon gaining earthly riches, feeling that he could never punish himself sufficiently for his great sins. Once he was upon a journey which led him through some estates which had once been his, and such an intense desire to humble himself filled his heart, that he insisted upon his companions dragging him by a cord through all the villages of that district, beating him severely, while they spoke to him in harsh and insulting words. His friends obeyed his commands, and the people were not only astonished by this strange sight, but also full of admiration for one who could thus publicly humble himself for his former sins, and many were led to deplore their own wickedness, and to set about amending their own lives in imitation of his example. Thus Giovanni travelled about, always preaching penance and poverty and the love of Christ crucified, until he was directed by God to return to Siena, that he might found a convent for religious women there. Afterwards he journeyed to meet Pope

Urban with his company of poor brethren, now more than seventy in number, and when they had made known to the Holy Father their way of life he promised them the religious habit. They were full of joy at this prospect, but God first allowed them to be tried by suspicion and evil report; many seeking to persuade Pope Urban that these poor men were touched with heresy, and saying other slanderous things about them. They were then strictly examined as to their belief in the Catholic Faith, and the Holy Ghost so enlightened and assisted them, that the Cardinal who questioned them was full of admiration, and invited them as guests to his own table that day. So the Pope gave the religious habit to Giovanni Colombini and his followers, counselling them to persevere faithfully in the life of holy poverty and penance which they had entered upon.

For a few days the brothers remained in Viterbo, that they might more fully understand the will of the Holy Father regarding the rule they should adopt, and then they took their way to the Lake of Bolsena, where they rested at a convent which is there. It happened, however, on that very day that Giovanni was seized with fever, and fearing he should grow worse, they carried him to Acquapendente, where everything was done to cure him, but all in vain, for his illness grew worse and worse, so he begged that a priest might bring him Viaticum.

After he had received the Body and Blood of Christ with faith and love, Giovanni was taken to the Abbey of S. Salvatore, where he called together his spiritual sons, bidding them farewell, and entreating them with God's grace to maintain a spirit of charity and humility among themselves.

On the 31st of July, 1367, this holy man passed from earth to the happiness of heaven, to the great sorrow of those who had been his companions, who carried him to the Convent of Santa Bonda, where he had desired to be buried, the people coming out from their homes and following reverently the procession as it passed along. Then his wife, whom he had left for God, came to look upon the body of Giovanni, weeping bitterly because she knew the grave would soon hide his sweet and holy face from her view, and with sighs and tears he was laid to rest near the entrance of the cloister. Many miracles were afterwards worked at the tomb, and therefore the coffin was opened, and when the body of Colombini was discovered perfectly fresh and sound, he was held in such veneration that crowds of people flocked to the place to pray. The wife of this pious servant of God lived some years after his death, spending her days in works of charity, in the reading of spiritual books, and in prayer, and then she too was taken from this life, where she had suffered and sacrificed so much, and entered into eternal rest.

Blessed Sebastian Valfré.

SEBASTIAN VALFRÉ was born in a small village of Piedmont upon the 9th of March, 1629, and that same day he was made one of God's children by the Sacrament of Baptism. His was a good old family, but one so tried by misfortune, that at the time of the little boy's birth his mother and father were working hard for their daily bread. But though Sebastian was reared in the midst of poverty, he had from his earliest years a great desire to help every one in need, and if any poor person was sent from the door unaided he wept bitterly, so bitterly, that the neighbours would come to ask what was the matter, and often gave him the food for their relief which his mother could not bestow.

At ten years of age this boy fasted during the whole of Lent on bread and water, and at all times denied himself many of the little indulgences which came in his way so rarely. He was also a very obedient child, never requiring to be told of even a trifling thing a second time, because his delight was to attend to the first wish and word of his parents. One day Sebastian was left in the kitchen to watch some food which was boiling on the fire, yet in spite of all his care it boiled over, and was spilt on the floor. The little boy was very much troubled—in a poor home this was a terrible misfortune—and he knew how grieved his mother would feel at the loss; but he never thought of concealing what had happened, or even making excuses for himself, as most children would do. He almost expected he might be punished, yet when his mother came in he went towards her, saying directly, "Mother, if you like I am ready to be beaten, but the pot on the fire has all boiled over."

Argentina of course did not punish or scold

her little son, because she was a good woman, who rejoiced to see this proof of Sebastian's truthfulness and obedience.

As the lad grew older, he felt God's voice drawing him to the priesthood, but his parents had too much difficulty in providing food and clothing for their twelve children, to be able to place Sebastian where he could pursue the necessary studies. After a time an opportunity was found of sending him to receive a course of instruction, but his master with whom he lodged treated him very roughly, making him sleep in a barn, with very little to cover him. Through the nights Sebastian lay in cold and wretchedness, unable to take off his clothing, yet even when his father came to see him he made no complaint, and did not explain how it was he looked so weak and ill.

A boy who was one of Valfré's school companions had a quarrel with another, and his heart was full of revenge. Sebastian heard of this, and it made him very unhappy, because he knew how it must grieve the good God, and he thought he would try to make peace between the enemies. So he went to his schoolmate and asked him if he had said the Pater noster that morning. Cappello did not know his reason for putting the question, so he replied quite promptly that he had said it.

"Did you say it carefully?" then asked Valfré, trying to speak with great love and gentleness, lest he might give offence. The boy again replied that he had done so.

"Surely you did not notice those words of Christ, 'Forgive us our trespasses as we forgive them that trespass against us,'" added Sebastian, earnestly; and young Cappello was so struck with shame and repentance, that he quickly asked pardon of God, and was reconciled to the lad who had offended him.

Having overcome great difficulties, and studied hard to fit himself for the life he desired, Valfré had the great happiness of receiving the habit which those wore who were preparing for the priesthood, and in 1651 he was received into the congregation of the Oratory at Turin, where, as a novice, he set a bright example of humility and obedience. On the 24th of February, 1652, he was ordained a priest by his own bishop in Alba, but after celebrating his first Mass he returned to the Oratorians, to whom he was much attached. Father Sebastian still applied himself very much to study, but he tried to become a true priest, setting before him as a model S. Philip Neri, the father and founder of the Oratory. In the instructions and short sermons which were part of his duty to give, he had much of the winning sweetness which made S. Philip so much beloved, and it was a common thing to see persons moved to tears by his earnest words. At the beginning of his priestly life Father Valfré was so humble, that he feared to undertake the duties of a confessor, as he judged himself unworthy of so holy a ministry; but afterwards, when he yielded to the opinion of several learned and pious men, who advised him to undertake the care of souls, he was sought by crowds of penitents. God gave Sebastian a great power over the hearts of these people: both learned and ignorant, rich and poor, came from him with fresh sorrow for their sins and fresh purpose of amendment in the time to come, and many notorious sinners were drawn from the depth of wickedness to begin a truly Christian life. It pleased Almighty God to bestow upon this holy man that wonderful knowledge of what is passing in the hearts of others, which has sometimes been an extraordinary grace and help to those who have a great work to do in saving souls. He often clearly knew what the penitent had either forgotten or was simply trying to conceal, and saying, "Will you let me tell you of something?" would put clearly before the person the diseased state of his soul. The King of Sardinia took Father Valfré as confessor, and under his guidance gave proofs of an unusual degree of piety, which won for him the admiration of all his people. The royal princesses, his daughters, also looked to the holy priest for counsel, and many letters from them have been preserved by the Congregation, which show the respect and confidence which they felt towards their spiritual father. But while Father Sebastian had so much time employed in assisting and directing the great and noble, his chief love was for the poor, to whom he gave every spare moment. He also took great care of his own soul, striving that while he led others to God he might himself grow daily more conformed to the example of his Master.

One of the chief works of the Fathers of the Oratory is the preaching of God's word in their churches, and Sebastian Valfré entered into this labour with the greatest zeal. He preached in the church of the Congregation at least once a week, and was besides this always ready to take the place of any priest who was called away to some other duty. In poorhouses, prisons, and hospitals, Father Sebastian laboured to win souls to God, and many were the hard hearts which he softened, and the cold indifferent lives which his earnestness awakened to a more ardent love of Jesus. He delighted, too, in catechising the poor and young, going himself to seek out the country people and collect them into small chapels. No matter whether he had to bear the cold of winter or the burning heat of summer, he journeyed on foot in search of those whose souls were so precious in the sight of God.

A woman who had been under instruction gave up the good resolution of professing the Christian faith. Happily Father Sebastian heard of this, and, going to the place where she was, requested her to say a Pater noster with him. Having said the prayer, he drew close to the woman and asked her if she would be a Christian. "Yes, Father," she answered, "very willingly;" and without any further doubts or drawing back she made her profession of Christianity, and persevered in piety and virtue until a great age, when she died a happy and holy death. At that time the number of Catholics in the valley of Lucerne was small, but by his journeys there Valfré did so much good, that new churches had to be provided for those who were converted to the faith by his preaching. As the love of God burns more and more brightly within the soul, so must there increase displeasure with all that offends Him; and thus if Father Sebastian knew of any one who was doing wrong in thought, or word, or deed, he would shudder, from the horror he felt, and even became seriously ill if he was very much distressed. He had a great dread of venial sin, and he always tried to excite the same feeling in those under his care. His own nephew once was found out to have told a falsehood, and although it was not about a matter sufficient to make it a grievous sin, Father Sebastian reproved him most severely, and told him that he should never again set foot in that room if he repeated the fault. Neither could this holy man endure to see any persons idle or tepid who professed to be the friends of God; he would strive to rouse them to do something for their neighbours, saying, "One who loves God never says it is enough, but the more he has laboured the more he is ready to labour." He certainly carried out these lessons in his own practice, for even when he was old and weak, and people thronged his confessional, or came seeking advice or alms, he never complained of being too much disturbed, but found time and a kind word for each one, all for the love of his Master.

During Sebastian Valfré's lifetime Turin was shut up by a siege, and that was a time for fresh exertions to do good to others. He hurried to the wounded when they were carried to the hospitals, comforting them with the holy Sacraments, and he would even stand amidst the dangers of the streets, where he might at any moment be struck down in the continual cannonading, because he thought that there in the midst of peril the hearts of men might be more easily moved to make acts of contrition. A miracle happened one day in one of his errands of mercy when the Blessed Sebastian had gone to the Royal Hospital of Charity in company with a young cleric. They had entered a room through which was the passage to the place where the sick lay, and Sebastian was going on, followed by his young friend; but, after taking a few steps this student stopped, and, turning hastily back, just avoided falling into a deep opening, which was there because the building was yet unfinished. Pale with fright at his narrow escape, the young man looked for his holy companion, whom he clearly saw walking upon the air, as if it had been solid ground, and thus reached the sick rooms, to which he himself had to pass by a longer way.

Another day a priest named Garresio was walking through Turin with Father Sebastian, who suddenly stopped at the door of a house and exclaimed, "Garresio, make haste and go up to the garret of this house, while there is yet time." The priest, without pausing to ask a question, ran up to the place mentioned, and there found a poor woman lying upon a little straw, evidently in her last agony, with no one to assist her. Garresio instantly begged her to make an act of contrition, and he gave her absolution, upon which she calmly expired, at peace with God. He then went back to the street and rejoined Sebastian, who had remained there till his return, and who quietly said, " Now we have gained a soul we may pursue our way."

Many such cases happened which showed the great graces God had bestowed upon this holy man as a reward for his faithfulness; many, too, were the miraculous cures he wrought, not only of the soul, but also in the bodies of those who came to him for help, and in spite of his many illnesses and great weakness, he seemed to receive from heaven power to toil on as many a stronger man could scarcely have done. When, however, the time of his death drew near, blessed Sebastian had a distinct knowledge of the day it should happen, and for some months he occupied himself in setting all things in order. In December (the last month of his life) he visited some of his friends, bidding them farewell as for the last time. Two days before he took to his bed he told a person in the confessional that he should never hear her confession again, as within a week he should be dead. The woman was greatly distressed, and cried out, "What can I do when you are gone? who will help me as you have done?" But Father Sebastian comforted her by bidding her trust in God and the Blessed Virgin, who would, in answer to her prayers, take care that she should want for nothing. The holy man was not mistaken, for his knowledge had come by God's revelation. After a short illness he died peacefully upon the 30th of January, 1710, having reached the age of nearly eighty-one years. When the news was made public, crowds of people went to the church, crying, "A great saint is dead." All wanted to see him who had been their patient loving father and friend, to kiss his hands and feet, and, if possible, cut off little morsels of his vestments, so that the Fathers thought it would be necessary to call a guard of soldiers to their aid, but all was in vain. The crowd thickened and would not be kept back, and so an order came from the archbishop to permit his body to be exposed for public veneration until late in the evening. The coffin was afterwards closed and sealed, and carried to the place appointed for the sepulchre of the Fathers of the Congregation; and many miracles were granted by God after the death of His servant in answer to those who asked his intercession to obtain for them Divine favours.

Blessed Imelda.

OUR dear Lord, when upon earth, called little children to come close to Him, He put His hands on them and blessed them, saying, "Of such is the kingdom of heaven;" and since then there have been many of tender age who have been drawn to Jesus by His sweet words of love, and have followed Him faithfully all their lives, until He took them to bloom like pure sweet flowers in the heavenly garden, where He keeps them safe for ever.

One of these children was Imelda Lambertini, whose home was in the city of Bologna, and though it is so many years since she lived and died, she is not forgotten, but is considered to be the special patroness of all first communicants.

As a young baby, her tears could always be dried by hearing the Name of Jesus or of Mary, and when she could speak she loved to lisp little prayers and repeat words from the Psalms, which were taught her by her mother in a small oratory which she had begged for her own use.

Some of those who have written the short history of little Imelda have thought that she died as early as the age of seven, but those accounts which are generally said to be most correct tell us that she was several years older before our Lord called her away from this world. So at ten years old we find that this pious little girl had a great wish to be placed in some religious house, where she might be near Jesus, be taught about Jesus, and prepare to belong to Jesus entirely when she grew old enough; and her parents very willingly granted her desire, and asked the Dominican nuns at the convent of S. Mary

Magdalen, in Valdepietra, near Bologna, to receive Imelda. In those times it was a common thing to allow children who were preparing to become Religious, or who had that wish in their hearts, to put on a habit similar to that worn in the convent by the nuns, so Imelda was given her little white habit and scapular; and as she looked at it, it always seemed to remind her to get herself ready to make solemn promises to be a spouse of Christ when she was older.

The little girl was very faithful to the rule she had to keep. We hear that she was never careless or indifferent about the smallest things which were required of her, and she had also a great desire to practise penance whenever she was permitted. Her great love was always for the Blessed Sacrament. Before It she was never weary, and every moment which was free she spent in prayer, kneeling so still that her whole heart seemed away from the world and all around her, wholly fixed upon Jesus her Lord and her King. This great deep love for the Blessed Sacrament caused Imelda to burn with desire to receive It in her heart, and when others knelt round the altar, tears filled her eyes and rolled slowly down her cheeks as she murmured, "When, ah when will He come also to me?" The nuns knew of the longing of the child's heart; they knew, too, her purity and piety, which seemed to make her fit to be a little temple wherein God might dwell; and yet in that country First Communion was fixed for the age of fourteen years, and they could do nothing to help Imelda, only bid her love on and pray while she waited. The little girl tried to bear the pain this caused her. At holy Mass she thought of the sufferings of Jesus, and begged Him to help her to bear to be kept away from receiving Him in the Blessed Sacrament; yet the longing God had implanted could not be kept down, and as the nuns and the other older children rose and knelt for Holy Communion, Imelda felt as if her heart must break with sorrow and with love. Thus time went on until Ascension Day, in the year 1333. The child was twelve years old only, and still she must pray and wait. It seemed that morning as if she could bear no more such suffering. With her small hands pressed tightly together under her little scapular, she bent her head down upon her breast and prayed, "Oh, sweet Jesus, Thou didst call children to Thee when on earth, Thou didst not turn them from Thee! Let me come. I love Thee so! I long for Thee so! Why, oh, why must I wait?"

No one there knew how the child prayed, how much she suffered, but God in heaven looked down and saw it all, and He would not delay His answer to such fervent prayers.

There were children going to the altar for the first time that day, and one by one they left their places with soft hushed steps, and, kneeling, waited for the coming of Jesus.

Far down the church knelt Imelda, her head bent low, to hide her streaming tears. The priest, turning, lifted up the Sacred Host, saying, "Ecce Agnus Dei. Behold the Lamb of God. Behold Him who taketh away the sins of the world;" and even as he spoke a bright golden gleam shot from the Blessed Sacrament, and passing down the church as a ray of light, rested upon the head of the little sorrowing, loving Imelda. Every one gazed with wonder. Then, with greater awe and greater wonder, the priest saw that the Sacred Host had left his hand, and shone like a star in the centre of the golden brightness which gleamed around the child. Her eyes were raised to look at the lovely star, *she* knew it was Jesus who had heard her cry, and had come in answer to her prayers.

The priest left the altar — the kneeling children made way for him, hushed and almost frightened at a thing so strange, and following the ray of light, he came to Imelda, and with trembling hands gave her the Blessed Sacrament, which was as a star above her head. The Communion was given, the Mass ended; many were leaving the church, and yet Imelda knelt on, and the nuns thought that it was not strange to see her thus rapt in prayer and thanksgiving. They let her be for a while, until her excessive pallor made them afraid she was fainting, and they sought to rouse her. In vain—the usually obedient Imelda heeded neither entreaties nor commands, but remained still upon her knees, with bowed head, and hands clasped above the little breast which held her Jesus. Then the good sisters were still more anxious and afraid, and they lifted her from the place. Ah, the gentle little girl was dead! Like Mary her mother, she had died from love, and her happy soul was with Jesus for ever.

In the year 1566, the Dominican nuns left the convent of Valdepietra, to establish another in Bologna, and to their church the remains of Blessed Imelda were removed. In the time of Pope Benedict XIV., one of her descendants, Cardinal Lambertini, embellished the grave where she was buried, and others of her family, in the year 1591, caused the miracle which closed her sweet short life to be engraved upon the stone above her sacred relics. And now in the present time many children in our own country have learned to know and love little Imelda. Like the little girls of Bologna, they choose her as their patroness, and pray that she will ask for them some of that love which burned so brightly in her heart, and especially should she be invoked by those who are preparing to receive our Lord in Holy Communion. We may not wish, like Imelda, to die in that moment of joy when Jesus first rests within our hearts—rarely indeed would God choose out a child for so great a proof of His Divine favour—but we must wish, if we cannot die for our most dear Lord, that we may live for Him, that our hearts may glow with love and longing to receive Him there, and that He may dwell within us always, never, never to be driven out by coldness or by sin.

Blessed John Berchmans.

IN the old town of Diest there dwelt a Flemish family of gentle birth, who were honoured and beloved by all the inhabitants of that part for their goodness and piety, and at the close of the sixteenth century a son was born in their house, whose holy life was to make the name of Berchmans dear to every Catholic heart.

The day following his birth, the infant was taken for baptism to the parish church, when he received the name of John, and the old baptismal register may yet be seen, although the church has been shattered by wars, its altars desecrated, and the building with difficulty saved from destruction.

At a very early age this little boy showed

great sweetness of temper, and God's grace abiding in his heart helped him to check a natural impulsiveness, so that he became strangely patient, and never seemed disturbed by the little disappointments and vexations which must happen in the daily life even of young children. When he came running home from school, if his knock at the house-door was not answered directly, instead of repeating it hastily or loudly, he would go quietly into the church of S. Sulpice, which was close by, and kneel down before the statue of the Blessed Virgin, taking the opportunity this delay had given him of saying a rosary, or even several, in her honour. At seven years of age the child was up at break of day, to serve one or two Masses before it was time for school; and once when his old grandmother grew disturbed at this practice, thinking it would injure his health, little John said to her, "Oh, I must serve my Masses before it is time for my lessons. Where could I better win knowledge?" Excepting to go to church and school, the child never cared to walk about the streets; his whole heart was given to the service of God, and to the studies which were better to fit him for his work, wherever the Divine Will placed him.

When John was nine years old his mother was seized with a serious illness, which kept her suffering for a length of time, and one of her greatest comforts was to see the smiling loving face of her little son constantly by her side, doing all that he could to relieve her, and speaking so sweetly to her of the love of God, that his words seemed hardly those of an earthly child.

As he grew older, the boy made rapid progress in his studies, especially in Latin, but although he surpassed his companions, no trace of pride was to be seen in his glance or bearing, no boastful word was ever heard to escape him. He felt that his abilities were but God's gifts, for which he must one day render an account, and therefore the progress he made and the approval which he gained were but to him the occasion of greater desire to do all things with the purity of intention which is so pleasing to the Almighty.

It will not surprise us to find that Berchmans longed for the happiness of becoming one of God's priests, and this wish, added to the report his master gave of him, made his father give a glad consent, and arrange to place the lad under the care of Father Peter Emmerich, a monk who had exchanged the cloister life for the work of a pastor, as the rule of S. Norbert permitted him.

Several other boys were dwelling with the good Father, all looking forward to the priesthood, and John found his new home a very happy one. In those times there was a custom at Diest to clothe some child in the vestments of a priest upon the Feast of the Holy Innocents, and allow him to take his part in the church offices, and the first year the choice of Father Emmerich fell upon John, who, it is said, sprinkled the holy water, incensed, and sung the collects in Latin, as perfectly as if it had been a familiar practice. It seemed from that day that a greater reverence and seriousness filled the heart of the boy, as if he better realised the dignity of the priesthood; and although he had ever been a respectful pupil, he redoubled the obedience and honour he had given his master, regarding him entirely as the minister of God. John was a cheerful merry boy, and yet no one can remember hearing him give way to loud laughter. He talked little and very carefully, lest he might offend with his tongue, and his greatest pleasure was to sit in silence, listening to the words of Holy Scripture, or reading lives of the Saints, or books which treated of the Sacred Passion. No boy amongst that little party was so useful as young Berchmans: indeed, his desire for lowly offices was such, that he tried to do a great part of the servant's work, and with a book in his hand seated himself close to the door, that he might open it at the ringing of the bell. It is said, though, that sometimes he was so absorbed in his studies that the familiar sound ceased to arouse him until the call was repeated.

Meal-times were times of very little satisfaction to John; he never seemed to consider what was offered him, never complained, or showed any taste for particular dishes, and he ate but a small quantity, so that the other lads would joke with him, asking if his mind went off travelling while he sat at table. But no laughter made him vexed, and even if any one attacked him with unkindness (a rare occurrence, because he was beloved by all), he bore it with quietness, as if he did not hear what was said.

Perhaps some one may ask how all this could be — how a boy could practise such constant charity and sweetness, and keep so free from faults which are common at his age. We shall find that the secret lies in his love of prayer, that fervent, trustful prayer to God by which he obtained the grace which was his strength and safeguard.

After a merry game with his companions John would silently vanish from their midst, and perhaps be found long after in some quiet, unfrequented corner, his whole heart laid open to God, his petitions, his fears, his temptations, poured out into the ear of that dear Father in heaven. One day, after long search, they found the boy in a box, just big enough to contain him, where he had been concealed at least two hours. Often he would kneel so long by his bed-side that sleep overcame him, and he would lie down in his clothes to take the needful rest.

It was between the age of eleven and twelve that John made his First Communion, and after a careful confession of his young life—which showed the purity of his soul so clearly that the priest who heard it doubted if there was sufficient matter for absolution—the boy gave himself wholly to prepare for the coming of his Lord in the Blessed Sacrament. His prayers ascended to heaven with increased fervour, his heart burned with desire to receive that Divine Guest, and with tears he besought God to empty his heart of all, so that Christ alone might reign there. And thus the great day came, and with downcast eyes, but with face glowing with holy love and desire, the little lad received Jesus his Saviour.

After that time John went each week to confession, and twice in every month received Holy Communion, and his piety and devotion grew sweeter and stronger under the influence of the Divine Presence in his young heart.

John was especially a lover of Mary, and she seems to have made him in a singular way her own child, for the greatest events of his life always happened upon her festivals; and in return for all the graces obtained him by this dear Mother, he paid her all the loving homage which is her due. If he used his pen as a youth it was in her honour; if he spoke of her there was a light upon his face, and a thrill in his voice, which revealed the devotion of his heart. If he passed any statue of her he saluted her with a prayer, and knelt before every altar dedicated to her name. Nor did he only offer his love to Mary; he also gave her penance, often depriving himself of pleasures, and still more frequently of food, in her honour, and therefore it is not strange that this Mother most amiable gave him love for love, and shielded him from the faintest breath which might injure the innocent purity of his heart.

Meanwhile the Father of John Berchmans was surrounded with many cares and anxieties. The Flemish families, however good their birth, were not ashamed to engage in trade, and the elder Berchmans had long been a thriving cordwainer, but bad times had begun for him, and the long illness of his wife brought him heavy expenses, which narrowed his means; so at length, when John was past thirteen years of age, he was sent for from school to hear the terrible news that his hope must be given up, and he must set himself to learn some good trade, as a means of support. Poor boy!—the blow was heavy, and for an instant its crushing weight stunned him. Then he knelt at his father's feet, sobbing and stretching out his hands, as he begged to be allowed just for a few years to continue his studies and enter the Church. "God calls me, father," he cried. "I feel it, I know it, and how can I give Him up? Do not hinder me, and I will cost you so little that you shall not suffer. Bread and water are all that I require—only hear me, and grant my request." The father's tears flowed fast, and the mother's voice was shaken with emotion as she raised her boy from the ground, and promised him that they would try and think of some way by which they could manage to yield to his wishes; and after a short delay they found a priest of Diest who offered to continue John's education free of charge. Very soon an opportunity occurred for the boy to be received in the house of a canon at Mechlin, where in return for some services he could obtain his board and schooling without expense; and much as his friends grieved to lose him from his native town, it seemed that God's Providence drew him away from home and the parents he loved so fondly. It was early in 1614 when John set off for Mechlin, to find a home with Canon John Froyment, who soon learned to love him as if he were his own son. The lad's especial duty was the charge of three little children, all brothers, who were pupils of the canon. He helped them in dressing, taught them their prayers, took them to Holy Mass, and watched over them with the greatest affection. Besides all this, Berchmans, considering himself a servant of the house, engaged in the most menial offices he could find, sweeping the yard and washing the dishes in the scullery, excepting when the canon interfered; yet in the midst of these common duties he always found time for prayer, for every action was in itself a prayer, because the thought of God was always before him, and everything that occupied him was a means of turning his heart heavenward.

During this time John's progress in study was rapid. He never lost a minute of the day, and managed always to have a book with him, which he might turn to if he had a moment free, and thus he soon rose to the head of his class, carrying off the first prize at the close of the year. There was a college of the Jesuits at Mechlin, and John felt himself irresistibly attracted towards it, as if God was indicating that it was his true place, and it was with great delight that he passed into it, taking leave of the seminary where he had first been placed. He now redoubled his zeal for study, and his success, combined with his sweetness of character, soon gained him the respect and affection of all his companions. Although he was only a day-scholar, he followed the smallest desires and orders of the masters, and would never join in a game which they did not fully approve.

A congregation or sodality of the Blessed Virgin had been established in this college, and the members were glad to receive Berchmans among their number, for they rightly guessed that he would be to them all a model of piety and humility. The love John had ever felt for Mary increased daily; he recited her Office prostrate on the ground; he fasted every Saturday in her honour, as well as on the eves of festivals, always adding some humiliation to his penance; and his fervour becoming partly known to his superiors, they reverenced him almost as a saint. As time went on Berchmans felt more and more desire to enter the Society of Jesus, and in order to be enlightened by God as to his vocation, he used to offer his communions for that intention, and prayed earnestly that he might know and do the Will of God alone; and when at length he felt sure that a Divine voice called him to enter the Society, he set himself to overcome every hindrance which rose up in his way. After much opposition from his father and friends, and many a struggle and storm to fight through, he was victorious at last, and on Saturday, the 24th

September, 1616, he presented himself at the door of the Jesuit novitiate when he had just entered upon his eighteenth year.

The story of John Berchmans' life as a novice is very beautiful — beautiful because of its simplicity and perfection — but we can only glance at it now. His exact fidelity to the rules was something remarkable, and he was looked upon as a model sent by God as a help to his companions. He was sweet and gentle, yet innocently gay, and every new comer was attracted to him by his kindness of disposition. No one saw him impatient, no one saw him angry, and yet he was so humble, that he begged three or four of his fellow-novices to watch him carefully, and tell him of every fault.

After the first year John was placed in a position which gave him some power over his companions, and made it a duty to report any fault in them which he observed; and this was a cause of great distress to him. Still, as obedience required it, he never shrank from speaking when it was necessary; but first he would go and pray for some length of time before the Blessed Sacrament, so that he might not act in haste. Every hour Berchmans recollected himself, repeated an Ave, and then said, "O good Jesus, Thou wast scourged for my sake; what have I done for Thee in return for such great sufferings?" And he would for a few seconds examine into the way he had performed each action, and make resolves to amend all in which he saw imperfections; and if any one chanced to be with him when the clock struck, he begged them to excuse him for a moment, and, without any human respect, knelt down and quietly performed his little hourly devotion, resuming the conversation afterwards with perfect simplicity.

At least seven times every day John visited the Blessed Sacrament, and he would gladly have lingered there if his duties had not called him away; but when he felt he ought to leave, he prayed that S. Aloysius and

S. Stanislaus would adore his Lord in place of him.

On Sundays and holidays, in the company of a lay-brother, John went into the villages near Mechlin to teach the catechism to the country people, and little children crowded round him, to whom he explained the rosary, and taught them to say their beads in honour of Mary.

Shortly after young Berchmans had entered the novitiate his mother died, and this sorrow had the effect of making his father desire to separate himself from the world, and give the remaining years of his life to the service of God as a priest. He did so, and thus the difficulties which had hung over John's path were cleared away, and he was able to make his first vows and publicly enter the Society he loved so much. This obliged him to leave Mechlin for Antwerp, that he might begin the necessary course of study. From Antwerp he passed to Rome, and in both these places, as in Mechlin, he was never known to break his rule; his modesty, obedience, and humility were sweet and constant lessons of perfection to all around.

He had many favourite maxims, all showing his very great love for the virtue of humility, and his desire to possess it; and he did not rest in the wish, but planned out a regular campaign against pride, seeking out practical ways of humbling himself. "The beginning of all sin is pride," he wrote at the head of one of his papers, and this knowledge kept him ever watchful, ever earnest in aiming at the virtue he loved, and which he possessed in so high a degree.

John Berchmans has left behind him many a note of his particular examens of conscience, rules by which to practise charity, obedience, and other means of arriving at perfection, and he wrote down stories of the Fathers about the Blessed Virgin and the Saints, which had a special interest in his eyes. Besides these, his method of preparation for confession and communion have been carefully preserved, every word of which breathes forth the most ardent love of God, the deepest sense of his own sinful nature. Many times it flashed upon the minds of those who knew and loved John, that his was one of those souls which God does not leave long on earth, and in the summer of 1621 he himself seemed filled with an ardent desire for death. Though his body was in this world, his heart was in heaven, and thus it was when the 31st July came, and the tickets for the patron saints of the coming month were given out, Berchmans read upon his paper S. Mark's words: "Take heed. Watch and pray, for ye know not when the time is;" and in a moment he felt that this was a message sent for him, and, full of joy, he told the glad news. A few days after, on the feast of "Our Lady ad Nives," he was slightly unwell, but this did not prevent him spending the holiday with the others; and on the following day he was engaged as usual in his studies, but at night an attack of fever set in, and he was seriously ill and was ordered to the infirmary.

Each day he grew a little weaker, although he remained cheerful and uncomplaining, speaking to those who visited him of the joys of heaven. When told that he should receive Holy Communion as Viaticum, he was overcome with delight, and taking a crucifix in his hand, he cried: "My Lord, Thou art all I ever had, all I have in this life. Do not Thou thus, Lord Jesus, abandon me." While John rejoiced, the community were in the greatest distress as they heard that Viaticum was going to be given him—it seemed as if a blessing was vanishing from their midst—and with tearful eyes they hastened to the room where the dying youth lay serene, and quiet, awaiting the coming of his Lord. But it was not until the morning of the 13th of August that his friends gathered round to see him die. In the night he had asked for a rule-book, which he took, and placing it with his crucifix entwined them both with his rosary and clasping them thus to his heart, exclaimed: "These are my treasures. These are the arms with which I defend myself against my enemy." As day dawned there were signs that the end drew near, and after receiving the last absolution he lost the power of speaking. His confessor told him to repeat the Name of Jesus with his heart if he could not with his lips, but making a violent struggle, he succeeded in saying it, until at last he quite regained his speech. The Father at his side then began to repeat the Litany of the Blessed Virgin, during which John gazed upon her picture with reverent love, and just at eight o'clock that morning of the 13th August, his soul passed from earth to heaven as his dying lips spoke the names of Jesus and Mary.

Many people flocked to the tomb where this holy youth was buried, kissing it with reverence, and covering it with flowers, and the devotion to his memory spread farther, so that in time his virtues were brought to light, and after receiving the title of "blessed" in 1865, his remains were translated to a fitting shrine, facing the altar-tomb of S. Aloysius—the saint whom he had taken as his special model, and whom he so much resembled in purity and sweetness. In the life of John Berchmans, we see no startling acts of penance; there is nothing to fill us with that awe with which we must sometimes think of the heights which Saints have reached. It is but the lesson we all know so well, yet practise so imperfectly—that fidelity in little things will win us fresh gifts of God's grace, and lead us to true sanctity at last. In the ancient town of Diest there is a house still standing, upon the front of which a niche is carved, wherein is the statue of a young man in a religious habit holding a book, a rosary, and a crucifix within his clasped hands, and underneath is the inscription: "The House of Blessed Berchmans." That book of rules he kept with such loving exactness, the rosary of the Mother who won for him such graces, the crucifix from which he drew lessons of love and sacrifice, were—as John said—his "arms," which carried him safely through the temptations of life, and made him victorious in the hour of his early death.

Blessed Benedict Joseph Labrè.

THE holy S. Augustine used to pray, "Lord, grant me to know Thee and to know myself. To know Thee, in order to love Thee, to know myself, that I may despise myself." And these words were frequently upon the lips of Benedict Joseph Labrè, and God answered him by an inspiration which drew him to a life of singular poverty and penance as a means of crucifying all love of the world's esteem.

The parents of this holy man were not poor. True, they had fifteen children, of whom Benedict was the eldest, but by his trade as a merchant, the father gained sufficient to maintain his large family comfortably. On the 27th March, 1748, the little Benedict was baptized at the parish church of Amettes, in France, being then but a day old. From his earliest infancy it seemed as if the child was specially loved and favoured by God, his disposition was so patient, so sweet, so docile. To his pious parents then it was an easy and happy task to instruct him in the holy Catholic faith, for he not only listened attentively, but seemed in his childish way at once to put in practice the lessons which he learned; and this is wherein so many of us fail. We are taught the fear of God, we read and hear the maxims of our religion, we have before us the examples of our Lord, His Virgin Mother, and the Saints, and yet this good seed seems to drop into our hearts week by week and year by year, without ever springing up into those beautiful blossoms of love, humility, meekness, and fidelity, which God is watching for.

However, it was not so with Benedict Labrè. He was a good, earnest little boy, and had made such use of his mother's teaching, that at five years of age he was thought fit to be placed under the care of a priest who dwelt in Amettes. He soon learned to read and write well, and was so anxious to get on, that his master often had to restrain him. Other children were being educated with him, and to them Benedict was always kind, bearing meekly any injury done to him. Once a little boy struck him, but he did not complain, and when the master found it out and questioned him, Benedict tried to excuse the offence, saying it must have been done by accident. Naturally, boys are very fond of amusement, and these little fellows used to play and loiter about the streets when school-time was over, but Benedict walked straight home without loss of time, and resisted all the persuasions of his companions to do as they did. This child of six years had a horror of small acts of disobedience, quarrelling, untruthfulness, and such faults. To him they were not "little sins," as so many call them, but offences which were giving pain to his Lord, and which, therefore, were horrible to him. It is very possible that some of his friends would feel vexed and angry with his strict ideas of right and wrong, but at length they loved him all the more because he was so good, and his presence restrained their passions, while his example became to many a model which they would strive to imitate. The little Benedict already began to do penances, trying hard to keep them secret from all but God. He would creep quietly out of his soft bed and rest his head on a piece of hard wood, and take that food which he liked least of what was provided by his mother.

The child had made himself a small oratory, and at eight years old he would take a younger brother as server, and try to imitate saying Mass; not in jest, but with the deepest devotion of his little heart. It seemed, indeed, as if Benedict's young life was full of but one thought, the thought of God and His service. At all times in the day he loved to go to the church, either to pray silently in some retired corner, or to serve the morning Mass with his hands joined before his breast, his eyes cast down, and his whole heart fixed upon God. From five years of age he went regularly to confession, for he was so early filled with contrition for every offence, that he could not rest without receiving the pardon of Jesus. He loved to be at catechism, to join in the processions, and other offices of the Church, and thus his innocent life passed until his twelfth year.

At that age Benedict's good parents placed him under the care of his uncle, who was a priest, so that he might begin the study of Latin and other higher branches of learning, and for four years the boy applied himself to it with great pleasure. But at sixteen he began to have almost a dislike to study; not from indolence, but because his heart was turned to the knowledge of spiritual things, to the reading of books of devotion and the lives of the Saints; and, above all, he loved the Holy Scriptures, and for the rest of his life always carried a copy about with him. Benedict's uncle at first was much displeased at this sudden distaste for his course of Latin study, and ordered him to persevere in applying his mind; but though the lad tried to obey, he no sooner opened one of his books than the disgust for it became like a great weight upon his heart, and he longed more than ever to read only of Christ and His servants. At last Benedict told his uncle that he felt God did not mean him to pursue studies which would only be useful in the world, and he expressed a wish to go into a cloister—the one which he had heard was more austere than any, La Trappe. The uncle represented the hardships of such a life, he told him truly that many far stronger in health were unequal to it; but all this did not serve to turn Benedict from his wishes, although the time had not come for him to seek to enter the cloister for which he longed. So, with this strong desire and hope in his heart, the young Labré went through his quiet routine of duty under his uncle's control. He rose very early, that he might pray in the silence and solitude of the morning hours; he served one or two Masses if he had the power of doing so, or, if another was before him, he withdrew silently, bearing the disappointment with the sweetness of one who saw in it the Will of God; he employed himself as much as possible in spiritual reading, was frequent in his recourse to the Sacraments, and, withal, was so humble, that at fifteen or sixteen years old he would place himself among the little boys for catechism, as if he needed the same instruction.

When Benedict was eighteen his kind good uncle died, and he then returned home, to carry on the strict rule of life he had taken up. His great desire to enter La Trappe was still strong, but his parents refused their consent, until at last his patience and gentle persistence caused them to yield. Benedict was as much delighted as if he had received permission to enter some place of delight, and in spite of the inclement season he set out upon this journey of nearly sixty leagues. Arrived there, the monks would not receive him; they looked at his young frail form, and bade him return to his home, until perhaps at some future time he should be more fit for a life of austerity. Benedict was deeply grieved, but the love of God in his heart was so strong, that he felt quite sure this disappointment had come for his spiritual good, and with that confidence he could not murmur, but returned to Amettes quite exhausted by the length of the journey.

In less than a year the youth wrote to the Abbot of the monastery, renewing his request to be admitted, but he was again refused; so as his parents had given leave for him to join the Carthusian monks, Benedict journeyed to their house near Montreville, in the year 1767. He found from the Fathers that it was necessary for him first to pursue further studies, so for this purpose he placed himself for a time under the care of the priest of Auctri, and then again presented himself at the monastery of Chartreuse, because it was the desire of his parents, although his own heart remained steadily fixed upon La Trappe. For six weeks Benedict remained as a postulant at Montreville; but God was calling him to a different state, so that He gave him neither peace nor content in the life, and at last the Father-prior said to him, "My son, the Almighty does not design you to receive the habit of a Carthusian. Follow His inspirations, and leave us."

So Benedict left the monastery, feeling quite sure the Divine Will had been clearly shown in his regard, and, writing to his parents, told them that he should again seek admittance at La Trappe—the one Order which he desired to enter. But it was in vain. Perhaps God chose this way of perfectly annihilating Benedict's will and desire even for a holy life. The Abbot still deemed him too weak for such a severe rule, and, accepting the refusal with great humility,

Labrè went to the monastery of Sept Fontaines of the Cistercian order, where he was without difficulty received. Scarcely had he entered than he was seized with violent illness of body, and still worse distress of mind, and after six months it was thought right to send him away, as God showed so plainly that he was not suited to that life.

So Benedict had to put far from him all those holy desires for the silent and austere cloister life he had thought of and prayed for since his childhood; and saying, "Not my will, but Thine be done," he turned with more fervent prayer to God, Whom he implored to grant him a clearer light upon his future course.

Thus by these many trials and severe disappointments Almighty God led Benedict Labrè to the strange, almost repulsive life of a poor, dirty, miserably-clad beggar, one who was loathsome in the eyes of the world, but very precious in the sight of heaven.

The year in which he left Sept Fontaines,

Benedict started on a pilgrimage to holy places. He journeyed on foot, in ragged garments, bearing the severity of winter weather and the burning heat of the summer sun; going by lonely ways, where he met no other travellers, and thus was dependent wholly upon God for consolation. Whenever he came to a town or village, this holy man imitated the example of his Master, in doing good to the poor and sick and sorrowful, and at length his piety gained him such respect and admiration, that he became afraid lest pride and vainglory might enter his heart, and he departed from the company of men to seek more solitary places.

Eleven times he journeyed to the Holy House of Loretto, where he kissed with affection those sacred walls, and felt his heart inflamed with a greater love for Jesus and His Blessed Mother; and the priests who observed his devotion felt quite sure he was a very holy man, and gave him leave to enter whenever he pleased. So there he would remain, kneeling motionless in prayer, weeping tears of joy and gratitude that God should suffer him to remain in a place where the Mother of Christ had dwelt.

His food was any bread which was given to him, any cabbage-leaves, fruit-parings, or useless thing he might find in the streets; his clothes were rags, which were so dirty, that even people who felt kindly and charitably towards him hesitated to approach him, and even some confessors were compelled to forbid him to come to their confessionals, because their other penitents would not enter where a beggar so filthy had been seen to kneel. In this Benedict found his most severe penance; his poverty was his choice, for in his home he would have had every necessary comfort and convenience. The dirty rags which he refused to change were assumed, not because he was careless about cleanliness, but because he found in this way an extreme mortification, and a means of separating himself from the society and charity of those who might perhaps have taken some of his love from God.

It has been very different with many other saints. Poverty and penance they have sought and loved, but cleanliness has been as dear to them as to us, so that we need not think a state like that of Benedict Labrè is part of the practice of holiness and austerity. It certainly was right for *him*. Who can doubt it when they read how constant and how humble were his prayers to God for guidance, how faithful his resolve to subject his own will to the most holy Will of God? With a heart so disposed, it would not have been possible for him to pursue such a life had it not been the one path which was to lead him to heaven. We may wonder—we may not imitate him or any of God's saints, unless a Divine Voice speaks and says to us as to them, "This is the way, walk ye in it,"—but while we wonder, we may not condemn, but dwell more upon the humble, prayerful heart of this blessed man, which ever found peace and joy in God amidst all suffering, reproach, and contempt.

In 1782, when Benedict made his last journey to Loretto, he was observed to be more than usually thoughtful, as if he had some sweetness hidden in his heart which absorbed him wholly. The fact was that Benedict knew he was going to die before very long, and that knowledge made him so happy, that he was always thinking of it. His longing for God seemed to grow daily more intense, and he would frequently murmur, "Call me, that I may see Thee." His grief for what in his humility he deemed his many sins, became stronger than ever, and he approached the Sacraments still more frequently in preparation for death.

Early in Lent, 1783, this poor man looked like one dying, the very sight of whom moved all to compassion. In Holy Week he could scarcely support himself on his feet, and yet he would drag his poor weak body to the church, and kneel there for hours before the

Blessed Sacrament. At last one day a fainting fit obliged him to leave, and rest awhile on the church steps, and there a crowd gathered round him. A man named Taccarelli felt great pity for Benedict, and calling him by his name, said his house was ready to receive him. Doubtless God was the author of this compassion, for Taccarelli forgot the poor dying man's miserable condition, and raising him in his arms, bore him to his own home, where he was laid upon a bed in all his ragged clothing. A priest was sent for, who bent over the beggar and said: "Do you wish to make your confession? Is there anything that you want?" And with a great effort Benedict murmured faintly, "Nothing, nothing."

It was known that the holy man had received communion a few days before, but the priest wished to give him the help of Viaticum, but death was too near for him to have that grace. His teeth were set together, his eyes closed, and when they administered the

Sacrament of Extreme Unction Benedict was unconscious of all around. At eight o'clock in the evening they began to recite the Litany of the Blessed Virgin, during which his soul quietly passed away into the presence of God, at the very moment when the bells of every church in Rome gave the signal for the "Salve Regina." He was thirty-five years old when he died, and in those years his soul had been his one great care. For that he had given up the world, with all its enjoyments and pleasures; for that he had neglected his poor suffering body; and now, as his reward, God took that pure soul into His own keeping, while even his wasted human form was to be honoured upon earth. People who had shrunk from the beggar of Rome came eagerly to look upon his calm sweet face in death; the clothes, which just before none would have touched, were begged now as precious relics; the bed upon which he died, the room where he lay, were visited with reverence by persons of the highest rank; and he was known at last as one of God's true servants, one of those whose humility has drawn down Christ, the lover of humility, to dwell in their hearts, and fill them by His sweet presence with all virtue and all grace.

Louisa de Carvajal.

SOME centuries ago, when London prisons were filled with priests lying there under a charge of treason for celebrating Holy Mass, when banishment or martyrdom would be the certain sentence of any who were convicted of being true to the Catholic Faith, which was hated and forbidden, a noble Spanish lady named Louisa de Carvajal left her native land, and risked the dangers and difficulties of travelling, that she might minister to the needs of the sufferers in England, and share, if God willed, in their persecution. This was no impulsive action. For twenty years she kept her strong desire hidden in her heart, until the time seemed come to make it known, and though her love for the persecuted and her sympathy with their sufferings might be partly guessed by the flushed cheek and sparkling eye with which she would speak of these confessors and martyrs, her desire was breathed out only in long hours of prayer to Him whose charity had caused Him to suffer and to die for men.

Louisa's parents were noble and rich, and in their ancestral home in the neighbourhood of Placentia she was born, and lived her first years of happy holy childhood. Very early, the little girl showed such a marked love for truth, that she was never guilty of even a shadow of deceit, and her patience and courage in any suffering were remarkable.

Visitors thronged to the house of Don Francisco de Carvajal, but his little daughter did not care to be seen by them; and there was often a struggle when her nurse attempted to dress her in rich attire and take her to the company.

Louisa's chief delight was with the poor. She loved to gather a party of hungry, ragged children round her, watching with delighted eyes their pleasure as she produced food and sweetmeats for them, and all the money she could obtain was distributed thus.

In this way six years of the little girl's life passed by, and then came her first great grief. Her father had removed his family to a colder part of the country, and the change brought an attack of ague upon Louisa, which caused her a long illness; but just as she was recovering, her mother was seized with fever caught from nursing a sick person, and in it she died a holy, peaceful death, commending her soul to God and her children to the loving protection of the Blessed Virgin.

Don Francisco was overcome with sorrow, and in his first agony of grief he resolved to consecrate the remainder of his life to the service of God, by entering the priesthood; but the Divine Will was otherwise, and within ten days he sickened and died of the same fever which had carried off his wife.

Louisa was now an orphan at but little more than six years old. Perhaps thus, and only thus, could she have been brought into such close union with God, and have learned the lesson of perfect detachment from creatures, which appeared in later days as the result of the trials of childhood and early youth. She was removed with her brothers to Madrid, where their guardians were living, but an aunt who occupied a high position at court wished to have charge of the little Louisa, and thus the care and affection which she needed were secured for her.

There was an elderly servant, Isabel Aillon, who went with the child to the palace, for to her care Don Francisco had specially commended his little daughter when he was on his death-bed. She was a good, virtuous woman, but of a harsh disposition, which was the cause of much suffering for Louisa, although she respected and liked Isabel because her parents had esteemed her. The child was much beloved in her new home, nor was she unhappy, yet she longed for her dead parents, and would go away quietly by herself to weep over her great loss.

Although she could not have the many opportunities of helping the poor which she had found in her mother's time, she had not lost her love for them, neither did she fail in doing what she could; and when some Religious came round to the palace, asking alms, Louisa would take from them the bag they carried, and go round to the ladies with it slung upon her shoulder, collecting what was possible.

The good Isabel Aillon taught her little charge a great many prayers, which she learned most readily, and repeated with marked devotion. She was especially eager to go to confession, and chose one of the Jesuit Fathers as her confessor, from which sprung up that strong love she always felt for the Society of Jesus. Isabel watched the child with ceaseless care, teaching her habits of self-control and modesty of manner, strictly forbidding any gossiping, and being very particular as to the books she read. With all these good points, the severe manner in which she punished the child's faults might be known by the black and blue marks which often appeared on her neck and arms; yet this extreme harshness served to teach Louisa patience in suffering, which was evidently what God intended her to learn.

At the age of eleven years, Louisa's aunt Doña Maria died, and then she was consigned to the care of her uncle, the Marquis of Almaçon, who received her into his family as one of his own children, and she was very happy there. But though she joined in the amusements of her young cousins, Louisa was serious beyond her years, and more and more of her time was given to prayer, because God filled her with so great a love for Him, that she desired nothing but to be in His presence, pouring out the desires of her heart. About this time she made her First Communion, on the Feast of the Nativity of

Mary, and she was so overcome with a sense of the greatness of Him Whom she was about to receive, that she trembled from head to foot as she advanced to the altar.

The Marquis soon found in his young niece such strong graces, such ardent desires for perfection, that he set himself to help her and urge her forward in God's service, and in return, her love and reverence for him were unbounded, so that she gladly obeyed the directions he gave her. The love to the poor, which had been in her heart from infancy, grew all the stronger as she better understood that in them she was ministering to Christ Himself, and she would give as long as she had money in her purse. She also managed to support two poor persons by depriving herself every day of the platefuls which were set before her, having taken one of the servants into her confidence, who quickly removed these supplies and made them over to her protégées. This was fully approved of by her uncle the marquis, and soon her cousins and her aunt began also to set apart some portion of their own meals for the sick and poor. The pleasure which Louisa took in visiting the hospitals was very great, and she would pass in and out among the sufferers, slipping fruit, biscuits, and sweetmeats into their hands.

All this time the love for prayer was increasing, and as she meditated on the sacred Passion of Jesus, the young girl thirsted for sacrifice, and felt as if she would gladly die for Him who had given His life for her; so that penances and mortification had an immense attraction for her, because, by this means, she seemed in a little measure drawn nearer to the way Jesus chose for Himself in the world. This attraction does not, however, appear equally in the lives of all the saints. It is one which is only given by God in a special manner to those who can by austerity better attain that patience, that sweetness, that courage and joy which will draw Him down to their souls in the wondrous communications of Divine love, and such an one was

Louisa de Carvajal. Her hours of sleep were curtailed, she knelt upon cold stones, to get the better of her drowsiness, her mattress was hard and unresting, and the hair-shirt, the discipline, the sharp girdle, were all to her so many helps to prayer, humility, and peace.

At about eighteen years of age Louisa subjected herself at her uncle's desire to a strange trial—she placed herself wholly under the control of two women servants, who were told to inflict upon her hard penances, and humble her in every possible way; and upon all this treatment she was to look as at so many marks of God's great love in permitting her to be conformed to the suffering and abasement of Christ.

The sweetness and courage with which Doña Louisa passed through this trial was wonderful: years after, she said that she could not have borne it if she had not had always before her the example of the meek and obedient Jesus, and the sufferings of His saints.

In this way years were passing on. The young Spanish maiden was entirely devoted to God, seeking only His love, putting far from her the world with its pleasures, and longing more and more for a life of poverty and penance, and yet, strange to say, she was conscious of no vocation to religion. "I wish with all my heart I was called to it," she would say to her uncle, when he represented it to her as the most suitable life for one who desired to keep retired from the world; "but I have never felt that God would have me to be a nun." This state of mind was difficult to understand, and the marquis asked the advice of many pious and learned persons, but Louisa's desire remained the same, and she felt drawn by the inspiration of God to a life of poverty and humiliation in the world — a life which would shut her out from the consideration and respect due to her rank, and which would also debar her from the reverence given to those who wear the habit of Religious, and seek in the stillness of the cloister a life of prayer and union with God.

At twenty-six years of age, then, Louisa de Carvajal began to follow the unusual vocation which was hers, dwelling in a small house, clad in mean attire, making herself one with her companions, who had been her servants, and sharing with them the menial work of their house. The rule of life adopted was strict, and their time was given to prayer, reading, work with their hands, and household duties. Louisa's great desire was to subdue in herself that natural sensitive pride of station, and the refinement which was part of her being; and for this end she subjected herself to great humiliations, begging bread in the streets of the city, and mixing freely in her shabby clothing with the crowds of dirty poor who thronged the steps of the churches.

At length came the time when God seemed calling her to the strange land of which she heard so much—that England to which for years her heart had been drawn with a desire few could have understood, to be among the martyrs, either to share in their sufferings by death, or to spend her life in serving them. Gradually her confessors, who had at first objected to her wish, began to believe it came from God, and she obtained leave to attempt her generous enterprise; and so, without shedding a tear of regret, Louisa de Carvajal left for ever her beloved country and all her friends when she was about thirty-nine years of age, undergoing the discomfort of the winter's snow and rain, and accepting any rough shelter which could be obtained as she passed upon her way, in the company of a chaplain, an Englishman and his wife, and two men-servants.

It was May before the travellers reached their journey's end, landing at Dover, from whence Louisa went to the house of a Catholic family, whom the Jesuit Fathers had prepared to receive her. It was one of the few homes which were left in peace just then, and Doña Louisa found herself free to enjoy the quiet retreat, where she could kneel in the chapel, in which several Masses were daily offered, and converse with pious persons and holy priests who were staying under that roof. After about a month's visit, the master of the house heard that he had been denounced as one who harboured priests, and that upon the next day his house would be searched; so, all in haste the pretty chapel must be stripped, and every trace of Catholic worship hidden, while the visitors dispersed in different directions, Louisa de Carvajal travelling with some other ladies in a coach to London. She stayed a few days in the house of a Catholic lady, where Mass was always said, and indeed afterwards, in spite of many changes and inconveniences, Louisa managed to secure this great help and comfort daily, receiving Holy Communion also. The time when this Spanish lady found herself in London, was the time when the discovery of the Gunpowder Plot had enraged all Protestants against the very name of Catholic, and when Catholics were alarmed at the thought of sheltering their own people beneath their roofs.

So the solitary stranger lived in hired rooms obtained for her through the kindness of the Spanish ambassador's chaplain, and there in the company of two English girls, who were both pious and good, she spent a year in perfect seclusion, practising almost the same rule of life she had taken up in Spain.

But even then she would venture out and visit the imprisoned priests, encouraging and consoling them to meet death with joy. The sufferings she witnessed must have been terrible, but perhaps still worse than the scaffold, and the blood, and the martyred heads fixed high on London Bridge, for the gaze of the Protestant crowd—yes, worse than all this, it must have been for her to see the unfaithfulness and falseness and sin amongst the people of Christ's own Church.

Great as had been Louisa's wish to aid the suffering Catholics, intensely as she longed to be one of those who shed their blood for the cause of truth and right, there were times when it seemed that she would have done better to remain in her own country, pursuing her life of prayer and penance, for she could not achieve her heart's desire to any great extent; yet when she prayed it seemed clear to her that God willed her to be in England, and therefore she remained.

Certainly her devotion to the Church inspired many a fainting heart with fresh courage and love; her fortitude nerved the timid to endure all that came upon them. Nor was this her sole work. She would speak openly about the Faith, and show the mistakes of Protestants with regard to it; and thus many were brought back who had wandered from the Church, and many by her means received the truth for the first time.

On one occasion her defence of the Faith in a shop where she was making purchases led to her being imprisoned, but the martyrdom she yearned for was denied, and she was released by the influence of the Spanish ambassador, in consideration of her being a foreigner, not subject to the laws of the king of England. In her own poor home she received all who needed shelter. At night she would walk swiftly to the secret hiding-place where a priest was concealed, perhaps only a few hours before he was seized and dragged to Tyburn, often taking with her some one who should receive from his lips God's pardon, and be made a child of the suffering Church.

It was, however, in the prisons that Doña Louisa's greatest work was accomplished, in those visits and consoling words with which she encouraged the captives as they awaited the terrors of a cruel death. Many of the martyred bodies were given to her care, that she might shroud them in linen ready for their burial, and she would preserve as many of their relics as she could, distributing such among good pious Catholic people.

In 1610 or 1611 Louisa's strength was so much exhausted by frequent illness that she was forced to remove to a house situated in what was then a country suburb — Spitalfields—which in our day it is hard to imagine as a "healthy open spot in the middle of a garden, separated on all sides from neighbouring houses." There she dwelt, with a number of young Catholic girls, who gladly sought her help and guidance, leading a life very similar to that practised in religious houses, looking up to her with the affection of children towards a mother.

Two years passed away in this quiet home. Doña Louisa seldom went out, and no longer visited the prisons, but Protestant feeling was strong against her because it was said that her house was in reality a convent, and therefore ten magistrates and about sixty men came to her dwelling, and, forcing their entrance, searched every apartment. Nothing met the eye but signs of great poverty, and they ceased their examination, but Louisa was arrested and carried to prison. She remained calm and peaceful, and when a priest hastened to visit her, she told him that all she desired was to receive Holy Communion, and in spite of the risk which she ran in thus communicating, she did so upon almost every day she remained in prison. The power of the Spanish ambassador obtained the release of Dona Louisa, and she, who would gladly have been carried from prison to the scaffold, was conveyed in the gilded coach which this friend sent for her; but the bad air of the cell in which she had been confined, and the cold she had endured, had been too much for her failing health, and she became seriously ill. It was soon plain that death was at hand, but Louisa was filled with peace and joy when she knew that God would soon remove her, and those who visited her upon her death-bed were astonished to see her so happy in the midst of such great suffering.

At the last she kept murmuring, "My Lord, what do I not owe Thee?" for the thought of the goodness and love of her Master made her own trials seem as nothing compared to the sweetness of His service, and thus, invoking the Names of Jesus and of Mary, Louisa de Carvajal passed from earth to the peace of the kingdom of God, upon the 2nd of January, 1614.

Claude and Marie de la Garaye.

A LARGE mirthful party set forth from the castle of La Garaye one autumn morning, to enjoy the pleasures of the chase, and first among them all was Claude Marot, the lord of that castle, with his young and lovely wife by his side. Theirs was a life which doubtless many envied. Rich, universally admired, and deeply attached to each other, it seemed that their happiness must be complete; and yet, with all its brightness, it was but a faint shadow of that greater happiness which God was preparing for them in a life of which they had not then dreamed, one which should be in Him and for Him only. But first must come a shock, a sorrow, and many a month of weariness and pain, for

God's voice is heard best in the silence of sickness or trouble, and when earthly hope is crushed for ever, the heart will turn for rest and peace to Him who has asked and waited for it in vain while earthly joy was brightest. That day, in taking a dangerous leap, Count de la Garaye felt that the ground on which his horse lighted was giving way, and, safe himself, he turned to warn his wife, but it was too late—the lady with her horse lay beneath the crumbling bank. She was not dead, as at first they feared. There was to be a long weary illness, and the knowledge that their one great hope of having a child to inherit their property could never be realised, and then once more their life went on outwardly the same as it had been before the accident of the hunting day.

But in their hearts both the count and countess felt that their joy was shadowed by the memory of their disappointment, and something seemed ever telling them that the pleasures of the world can never truly satisfy the soul, which is stamped with God's own likeness. However, they strove to content themselves with increased alms to the poor, and the assistance of all who were dependent upon them.

Early in the year 1710 the count and his wife were visiting a member of his family upon the occasion of a baptism, and in the midst of the rejoicings a young man who was among their friends died suddenly, without receiving the last Sacraments. This death seemed like a solemn warning sounding in the ears of the Count de la Garaye, and he sought the holy Benedictine monk who had been summoned too late to the side of his dead friend, and poured out to him the feelings of his heart, his yearning for a life which was higher and more satisfying than that which he had pursued.

It seemed to the young man then that in entering the married state he had deprived himself of those graces and joys which could be found only in the cloister, but the monk assured him that there might be peace and holiness and perfection found in other paths for those whom God has not called to the religious life.

"My son, wherever the Will of the Almighty appoints us to be, there we can sanctify ourselves," he said; and he departed, leaving the count to think upon his words.

A few days later the holy man received a message begging him to come once more to the castle.

"Father," said the count, "I have forgotten God, I have acted as if I did not believe in His existence: is it possible that He has borne with my neglect during all the years of my life?"

The monk comforted him with the assurance of God's infinite mercy and love, and besought him to believe that it was the Holy Ghost Which was now enlightening him; and then the count declared his purpose of devoting himself and all he possessed to the Divine service, saying that he would sell all and give to the poor, and serve them for the love of Christ. The monk was inwardly rejoicing at this generous intention, but he reminded M. de la Garaye of the difficulties which would arise, and also the necessity of gaining the consent of his wife.

They went to the apartments of the countess, and in the presence of the monk Claude told her all that God had been working in his soul, and he begged her to be his companion in penance and poverty, as she had been his companion in pleasure.

Marie was silently shedding tears as he spoke, and thinking her to be displeased, the monk hastened to assure her that her husband had no wish to compel her to accede to his desires, but that he would trust to the guidance of the Holy Spirit.

The countess rose and knelt at the feet of the priest. "These are not tears of sorrow, Father, but of joy, because to me also God has made known His Holy Will, and I thank Him that the same message has come to my husband, so that we may together serve our Master in the persons of His poor." Then, by the advice of the priest, Claude and Marie prepared themselves by a spiritual retreat for the life of penance to which God evidently called them, and from this they came out full of strength and courage to accomplish the Divine purpose.

The first care of the Count de la Garaye was to repair any injury he might have caused others in his pursuit of pleasure, offering to recompense all persons for harm done to their ground and crops in districts over which he had been accustomed to hunt. The next thing was to summon his large household, and inform them of the life which he and the Countess intended to adopt, saying that those only might stay in the castle who would labour with them in serving the poor. Three only out of the large number of servants were willing to remain. One of these was stationed at the gate as porter, with orders to refuse all noble visitors, but to admit every poor person who appeared. Then the lord and lady of Garaye sold the best part of their furniture, and all their splendid silver; their carriages, horses, and dogs went also, the jewels and costly robes which the Countess possessed were used for the service of the altar, and she, the delicate and lovely lady who had graced so many a ball and banquet, and rode so gaily to the hunt, now rose early to sweep and dust, while her husband occupied himself in splitting wood, drawing water, and laying tables for the poor.

Two or three hundred were fed at the castle, the count and countess helping to prepare their meals, and afterwards giving them religious teaching. Once a week they distributed money amongst the people of the adjoining town, and employment was provided for those who needed it. One of the first good works to which they devoted themselves was the establishing of a hospital for the sick poor, and many of the sufferers were lodged in their own castle until the building was ready.

About the close of the year 1714, M. and Madame de la Garaye went to Paris for a spiritual retreat, she retiring to a convent, and he to the monastery of La Trappe. After this they went through a course of study in those subjects which would prove useful in treating their sick patients, and then they returned home to work for Christ with fresh zeal and love.

New works of charity opened for them, two religious foundations were made, the hospital was completed, and then enlarged. Those children whose parents, though poor, were well born, even noble, were placed in convents for instruction; young girls whose want of means seemed to stand in the way of their vocation to religious life were assisted; the sick and sorrowful of every class were relieved and consoled, and thus the days of these two servants of God passed by for more than forty years. Then Claude de la Garaye became ill and weak, but no pain kept him from the side of his patients so long as he could get to them, and to those who begged him to spare himself, he would say, "Let me die amongst my poor."

In the autumn of 1754 severe illness attacked him, and after some months of intense suffering his physicians told him that recovery was not possible, but the holy man's face was bright with joy at this good news; the thought of being in God's Presence was for him perfect happiness. He was carried to the hospital for the last time on the 1st June, 1755, and there he helped his wife in portioning out the food for the patients, but in two days he was so much worse that it was judged well that he should receive the last Sacraments; yet he rallied again, and it was not until the 2nd of July that he passed gently away from this world, with whispered prayers upon his lips and a look of inexpressible peace and rest upon his face.

Marie de la Garaye was now alone, but no one saw her weep. She was not dead to human feeling, she was not insensible to her loss, but she had learned from God to be truly detached even from her constant companion—that beautiful detachment which is not coldness or indifference as some suppose, but simply means that the object of love can be given up without a murmur when God speaks the word. So though many noticed that the cheek of the lady of Garaye was paler, her step perhaps more quiet, her voice hushed and low, she was seen serving her poor as usual, and heard Mass in the chapel where the body of her husband was lying. "It is but for a little while that we are separated," she said, and in this assurance she found comfort.

It was as a poor man that Count de la Garaye was buried, but if there was no pomp or grandeur in his funeral procession, there were the widows and orphans and friendless whom he had helped in their distress. When all was over, and his body was lying in the burial-place of the poor, Marie de la Garaye returned to her course of daily labour and duty, waiting for the time when God should call her to her rest. Nor was it long. Only two years, and her remains were lying by the side of her husband's, and her soul we may believe was reunited to his soul in the bliss of heaven, while their holy memory was cherished by the peasants of Brittany, amongst whom they had lived and laboured; and the beautiful lesson of their devoted charity comes down to us in later days, proving that perfection does not lie in one path of life alone, but that in any state and any place our sanctification is God's Will, and His grace will be given abundantly if we are but faithful and generous in our love.

Madame de Miramion.

UPON the 2nd of November, 1629, Marie Bonneau de Miramion came into the world which smiled so brightly upon her future, which offered her its homage and flattery by right of her wealth and noble ancestry, which however was to be kept down under her feet by God's grace, as she passed through its allurements and dangers with a soul unspotted by its corrupting influence.

Being secretly convinced that she should not live to shield her daughter from the temptations which would surely come, the mother of the little Marie applied herself earnestly to instil into the child's mind that love of

God and virtue which alone could be her safeguard.

This presentiment proved correct, for when the little girl was but nine years old this good mother died, and her sorrow was so intense that she became ill, and it was thought that she too would be called away from earth. But God's purpose was to spare the young life, after teaching Marie in her illness and loneliness the great lesson that He alone remains our Guide and Friend for ever, and that all her heart must belong wholly to Himself. It seems that the sorrowful child turned to this good God and Father to help her in bearing her heavy load of grief, and as she regained her usual health, she set herself resolutely to practise all those lessons of virtue which had been taught her, setting that dear dead mother before her as a model for imitation.

M. de Rubelle having five children, several of whom were younger than Marie, gladly accepted the offer of his brother to join his household, and as the saloons of this brother's wife were frequented by the great people of the day, and a spirit of luxury and fashion prevailed throughout the family, the little girl found a great change from the quiet simple life she had passed by the side of her mother. Her aunt was a kind and loving friend to her, but being absorbed in worldly gaiety, she desired to train Marie to shine in the most polished circles of French society, and thus, through her very affection, she became one of the child's greatest temptations.

Marie, at twelve years of age, was allowed some small share in the balls and plays and fashionable assemblies which went on, and at first the novelty gave her a little pleasure, but she soon found that these things gave her no true and constant happiness, and she wearied of them all.

Fortunately the young girl had a governess whom her own mother had chosen for her as being possessed of true piety, and this lady endeavoured to foster these serious thoughts, and to impress upon Marie that they came from God as a check upon any temptation which the world might have for one so young. Although she danced beautifully, and was frequently taken to the crowded ball-rooms which her aunt attended, the young girl would wear a hair shirt beneath her jewelled robes, in order to keep herself in the recollection of the Presence of God.

Naturally she felt some attraction to the theatre, but although she never refused to accompany her aunt when she desired it, Marie resolutely closed her eyes and ears to all that went on, without attracting the attention of her companions. At this time she began to feel a great desire to nurse the sick, but being too young to visit them in their homes, she turned her attention to any among the large number of servants belonging to the family who required her help, taking the sufferers under her special care, making sure that proper medicines and food were supplied, and reading to them herself from spiritual books.

One Twelfth Night—that great festival of France—an old servant was seized with his last agony. Marie knew of this, and being missed from the gay party which had assembled, she was found at last, in her ball dress and jewels, kneeling on the floor by the bed of death, soothing, comforting, and praying for the sufferer, and refusing to leave him until all was over. After that she could not turn to amusement, but all unconscious of the sounds of mirth and music which filled the gaily-decorated halls, she spent the entire night in prayer in her own room, entreating God's mercy upon the soul which had just passed away.

Another great sorrow was coming upon Marie. During a brief absence from Paris in the company of her aunt, M. de Rubelle was taken suddenly ill, and before his daughter could reach him he was dead. As she wept over the lifeless form of her last remaining parent, the old lesson of childish days seemed freshly revived, and she comprehended more than ever the worthlessness of any love which is not fixed on God alone. Then the thought of entering a religious house first seriously occupied her mind, and she resolved that if she adopted such a life it should be in the Order of Our Lady of Mount Carmel, where she would offer herself to God. Marie spoke to her aunt and uncle of her aspirations, but they told her that she alone could supply to her young brothers the place of their lost parents, and that it was she who must be their shield against the evil influences of the society of the day.

Marie thought deeply over these words, she thought and she prayed; then, resigning her hopes of a religious life, she took up her work as the adviser and friend of her family, and thus became the tie which bound them together with unusual love.

The time came when Marie was sought in marriage by many men belonging to the most distinguished families of France, but she resolved that position and wealth must not influence her choice. She would not have consented to enter upon a married life had she not been told that it was God's Will for her, but she determined that her husband must be one who would help her to fix her soul above the things of the world. Gladly as she would have consecrated herself to God alone, true and ardent as had been her desire to embrace religious life, she put all these wishes and hopes from her, simply and humbly, as one who believed her path was leading another way; but the longing to trample on the world's pleasures, to follow Jesus in poverty and self-abasement, were all helps in enabling her to advance steadily towards the degree of perfection to which she was really called.

From childhood Marie had been accustomed to attend the services of the church of S. Nicholas-des-champs, and there too might have been seen the family of M. de Beauharnais Miramion, whose only son was one of the many who offered her marriage. His evident piety and goodness influenced Marie in making him her choice, and upon the 27th of April, 1645, they were married, she being then but little more than fifteen years of age. The next few months of her life were very happy ones; she was loving and beloved, and it seemed as if no sorrow could touch her any more. But when she was expecting with great delight the birth of a little child, her husband was attacked by fever, and after a short illness he died, leaving Marie a young widow. She had watched him and waited on him from the beginning of the disease, and when all was over she broke down under the intense grief, and fell senseless by the side of the corpse, remaining there for hours; and even after she was conscious again she seemed unable to cry or mourn, but lay in a speechless, stony grief, which was very distressing to the friends who bent over her. At length, after a time of weakness and illness, Marie's little daughter was placed in her arms, and then tears fell fast over the fatherless baby, and the necessity of watching over its life roused her from her deep dejection. For two years Madame de Miramion lived quietly retired from the world ; then she was once more in danger of death, from a severe attack of smallpox of the worst kind. But she recovered, and though the brilliancy of her beauty was gone, there was a sweetness upon her face which was perhaps as great a charm in this young widow of but seventeen years. Many urged her to a second marriage, but Marie besought her friends not to speak of such a thing to her, and removing to a country house in Normandy, she gave herself up to many hours of prayer, and the constant care of her little girl. It seemed to her that now she was specially called to minister to Christ in the persons of the sick and suffering, so she began visiting the poor in that district, dressing their wounds with her own hands, in spite of great natural dislike to such a task, which cost her many an effort to subdue.

The child whom God had given to Marie

de Miramion was so frail and delicate as to cause her constant anxiety, and, in fear of losing the little one, she made a vow to perform a pilgrimage to the chapel of S. Valerian, if it pleased heaven to spare her life, which was just then threatened by a complaint of the chest. Her prayers were heard, and the child struggled through the illness, so that the mother made arrangements to begin that pilgrimage which she had vowed to make, and for this purpose she started from Issy with her mother-in-law, attended by several servants. In those days the country was in a very disturbed state, and people were in fear for their lives if they travelled the smallest distance without a number of pages and men to guard them on their way; but Madame de Miramion proceeded safely until she was within a league of the close of her journey, when the carriage was stopped by a band of armed men, who, taking them prisoners, drove them off at a tremendous pace, they knew not whither. As they entered a gloomy forest, Madame de Miramion seized an opportunity when the door was unguarded of jumping out of the carriage, but her flight was discovered, and she was dragged back from the thicket of thorns and briars among which she had sought a hiding-place.

At length they reached a castle which belonged to a baron who desired to compel her to accept him as a husband, and every means of persuasion was tried to induce her to yield, but she only replied that her resolve was unalterable; and sending away one by one the choice dishes which were placed before her, she declared that she would not taste food until she was set free. Her mother-in-law, with the groom and maidservants, had been left behind in the forest of Livry, so that Marie de Miramion was alone, but she earnestly sought aid from above, and after some hours she was once more placed in her carriage and driven in the direction of the city of Sens. Then the horses were unharnessed, and she was left to get towards the town on foot, and being quite exhausted from terror and fatigue, she asked shelter in the first house she came to. Her request was granted, and a room was prepared for her, and then she heard that a troop of soldiers were hastening to rescue her, and that the whole town was disturbed with the news of her having been carried away. After such an accident, it was not strange that Madame de Miramion had a long and serious illness, and in the solitude of her sick room she had leisure to think more seriously than ever of God's claims upon her, and she resolved to go and stay awhile in some convent, that she might give some weeks to special prayer. It was in a house of the Order of the Visitation that she retired from her friends in the world, and there, in the midst of the hallowed associations connected with Madame de Chantal, Marie de Miramion thought once more of that life which had been her early dream and desire; but the wishes and needs of her near relatives seemed to make a barrier which

God permitted, and she believed it was His Will that she should live as a Religious in the world, giving herself wholly to His service, to prayer and penance, to humiliations and sacrifice, without the shelter of the cloister and the habit of a nun.

She was praying at this time before the Blessed Sacrament, feeling fears and doubts as she contemplated this difficult path, when God spoke to her by some interior voice, saying, "Am I not powerful enough to keep thee in any state I choose for thee? Fear no more, but give thyself entirely to Me." For hours Madame de Miramion remained lost in prayer, these Divine words had so penetrated her soul, and when the person in charge of the church roused her, she left the place with fresh courage and love. Once more she was praying there when the heavenly voice reached her again, asking for her heart. "Thy heart, my daughter, is the only gift I prize;" and after this she hastened to consult her confessor, who bade her make a retreat, that she might receive light to know God's Holy Will with regard to her life.

During that time of retirement she was roused from a deep sleep by a sharp blow, which caused her to start up, thinking one of the nuns had called her, but the room was lighted as if with the morning sun, and the same Divine voice she had heard before spoke clearly and distinctly, saying, "Be not astonished. It is I—thy Lord and Master—who addresses thee." Filled with loving reverence, she knelt upon the floor, while God gave her those counsels by which she was to be guided, and then the bright light passed suddenly away, and she spent some hours longer in fervent prayer. Upon the following 2nd of February, her director allowed her to make a vow of chastity, which bound her for ever to that Divine Lord who sought her heart as a precious gift, and from that moment Madame de Miramion gave up the silk and lace and jewels which had composed her usual dress, limiting herself to dark-coloured stuffs, as better suited to one who desired to be dead to the world. When people ridiculed her, she turned for comfort to a life of active usefulness; but her director checked her in these employments until she had learned greater knowledge of spiritual things by constant prayer, and after a year of the life of recollection and penance which he advised, this priest gave her leave to follow out those desires with which God had inspired her.

There was great misery in the land at that time, a time when charity was needed by the poor, whose country had been laid waste, and whose harvests had been destroyed by war. Many were suffering from famine, many from disease, and Madame de Miramion came to the help of all such, watching over the sick by night and day, feeding beggars at her own house, and selling her jewels to obtain more money for their relief. In towns and small villages she caused missions to be preached at her own expense, and in the neighbourhood of Paris she exerted herself in teaching catechism, and influencing men and women to fulfil their duty to God. The little child whose life had seemed so frail had grown old enough now to receive some education, and although the separation cost her much, Madame de Miramion resolved to place her under the care of the nuns of the Visitation. But she did not lose sight of the little girl. Three times a week she visited her, taking her to her country-house for air, and in these excursions she trained the child to visit the poor and sick of the village, denying herself some pleasure in doing so, that she might learn that true charity must bring sacrifice with it.

Then Madame de Miramion became the mainspring of all the great charities of the day, providing for the wants of foreign missions, assisting the priests who were going to preach Christ's gospel of love in distant lands, and yet never forgetting the claims of her own country.

One great need of Paris at that time was

some refuge for those who had been in prison, and who, when set free, often sank into crime because they had no home and no friends to help them. Madame de Miramion hired a small house, in which seven or eight such women could be received, and placing two trustworthy persons at the head, she tried to win them to virtue by kindness and religious teaching. This work grew until hundreds were under her care instead of some half-dozen, and her next public work was to establish a house for the instruction of young girls, where they should be taught work by which to gain a livelihood. The benefit of this home was so great, that her example was followed in other districts, and the king himself spoke approvingly of this benevolent scheme.

Thus years had passed, her duties to her child had not been neglected in the midst of works of mercy, but that child was now grown up and given in marriage, and Madame de Miramion was able to start a work which was very near her own heart after years of patient waiting. This was the assembling together of a few pious women, who should form a little community under the title of the "Sainte Famille," whose life was to be devoted to prayer, and yet who should be ready for any work of benevolence which sin, or sickness, or suffering might need. In a small house, therefore, this nobly-born woman commenced her little community, whose daily duty was the teaching of poor schools, or the visiting of hospitals and the poor in their own homes.

But to name every means by which Madame de Miramion brought souls to God and worked wonders for His glory, is not possible in so brief a history. She had laboured zealously in every work which was open to her, and as a reward even in this world God gave such peace and joy in her dying hours that those who knew her best marvelled because she had no fear of death, no shrinking from suffering. At first her constant vomiting made her confessor fear lest she should be unable to receive Holy Communion, but her Lord came to her help, and she afterwards obtained the grace of all the last Sacraments. Then, with radiant eyes, she prepared to die. "It is time to go to God, and to enjoy Him," she said, and then, in her humility, fearing she had spoken too certainly, she added, "At least, I hope so."

She suffered agonies of pain, but there was not a murmur. All was accepted sweetly and lovingly in union with the sufferings of Christ; and thus, with peaceful smiles and lips pressed fondly upon the cross, she passed away from this world which she had made her means of sanctification, living in it in bodily presence, and yet with a heart so wrapt in God, that neither pleasure nor power, neither influence nor esteem, could create one passing interest that was not in Him and for Him who was her life, her all.

VEN. ANNA MARIA TAIGI.

IN the world around us there are many persons struggling with the difficulties of poverty, who are loaded with cares and anxieties which seem to hinder them in the service of God. There are many who cannot offer Him a pure heart which has never been stained by sin, yet, in their grief for misspent time and neglected grace, would gladly atone for the past by fervent, grateful love, casting themselves upon the mercy of the Saviour; and to all such the life of Anna Maria Taigi is full of holy lessons of contrition, of patience, of the faithful discharge of daily duty, and of a spirit of humble, constant prayer.

It was upon the 30th of May, 1769, that she was born in the city of Siena, and baptised at the Church of S. John the Baptist there.

Her father was in business as a chemist, but when Anna Maria was about six years of age he lost all he had through his own fault, and having no means of living in Siena, he resolved to go to Rome, and his poverty was such that he, with his wife and little daughter, had to journey on foot the whole way.

Wishing to give the child a Christian education, her parents placed her in a school under the care of some nuns, and there she prepared to make her First Communion, which took place when she was about thirteen years old. The time had come then for her to leave school and assist her mother. The world seemed very bright and tempting, and she felt drawn to its pleasures, but Jesus and His Mother watched over the young girl, and preserved her from falling into any great sin.

In 1798 Anna Maria married Dominic

Taigi, who was employed in the service of a noble family, and although he was a man of good character, he had a disposition which was very trying to his wife, and gave her constant opportunity for the exercise of patience and gentleness.

But as soon as the marriage had taken place it would seem that Anna Maria forgot the teaching of earlier years, and gave herself up to the pleasures of the Italian people. Dress was the first object of her desire; theatres and other places of amusement possessed a charm which the practice of her religion did not then afford her; serious temptations fell across her path, and she did not seek God's grace to resist them. Conscious of her sinfulness and worldliness, Anna Maria was not happy. There were moments when she found distraction in pleasure which was sufficient to silence the pleading of the Holy Spirit, but God was too merciful to let her alone, and in His love He filled her heart with pain and remorse.

One day she was setting off to some amusement, dressed in very gay attire, when a holy priest whom she did not know met her in her way, and as she passed the voice of his Master seemed to say to him, "Dost thou see that woman? Thou wilt convert her, and she will be a saint." The priest was much struck by this occurrence, and pondered over the words which he had heard. But Anna Maria was as yet unconscious of God's purposes with regard to her, and some time had still to pass before she loosed her hold of the vanities of the world.

At last the day came when in her misery and remorse she resolved to begin a new life, and going into a church, she entered a confessional, and said to the priest who sat there, "Father, you see before you a great sinner." It seems strange to hear that the priest bid her leave him, saying that she was not his penitent, but thus it was; and Anna Maria, full of confusion and discouragement, went away: however the impulse of grace remained in her heart, and after some delay she went to another church, desiring to be reconciled with God.

Once more she entered the first confessional in which there happened to be a priest, but before she spoke he exclaimed, "So you are come at last." It was the Religious who had once met her gaily dressed for a scene of pleasure, to whom God had promised her conversion, though she knew it not; and now he told her what had happened to him, and the impression made upon her was so great that she generously gave herself up to her Lord, confessing every sin against Him with the deepest contrition. Thus Anna Maria Taigi found one who bestowed upon her the greatest care, helping her to practise virtue, as well as instructing her in the way of self-renunciation and sacrifice which God seemed calling her to pursue, and thus the apparent harshness of the priest who had refused to listen to her proved the means of carrying out the Divine purpose by leading her to another who could better undertake the guidance of her soul.

Anna Maria Taigi's conversion was thorough, and she wished at once to give up the fine clothing and ornaments which had been to her occasions of many temptations and sins; she longed also to practise severe penances in expiation of her offences against God, but in this her confessor frequently restrained her.

In reading the lives of the favoured servants of the Almighty, we cannot fail to be struck by the different methods by which He rules and guides them, and thus we find that Anna Maria had only just given her heart to God when He poured out upon her wonderful gifts and graces, which are often delayed till the later years of some of the greatest saints. Perhaps thus her soul was more penetrated with a sense of His great love—a love so undeserved by one who had neglected and turned from Him too long; perhaps this was her best preparation for the bitterness of desolation which was to follow. However, her intimate union with God caused such raptures of love, that she frequently appeared quite out of herself, neither seeing nor hearing any one who was present.

When Anna Maria received Holy Communion, her love for Jesus was so ardent that some sign of it would appear upon her face, and many persons observed her fervour, and would wait outside the church and ask for her prayers. Others called her a hypocrite, or said she was an enthusiast, and in different ways she attracted so much attention that she was obliged to make her Communions sometimes in one church and sometimes in another, until her Lord Himself made known to her that His Will was for her to frequent her own church and make no account of those who remarked her.

In the year 1799 the French had come to Italy to make it into a republic, and one morning the troops were hastily assembled in the square where the Church of Our Lady of

Piety was situated, and the noise and confusion caused all the people there to hasten home, with the exception of Anna Maria Taigi. The sacristan came to shut up the church, and found her motionless in prayer, giving no sign of having heard anything; and it was not for some time that she rose up, finding with surprise what had happened, and then passing quietly without any molestation through the midst of the French troops.

But although God gave His servant these favours in prayer, He soon called her to suffer for Him both pains of body and the far worse pains of soul which followed the sweetness of the days succeeding her conversion. Temptations to doubt her faith, temptations to hate God—in these and other such ways was the enemy of souls permitted to try her; but when her need was greatest our Lord always came to her help, and taught her to drink lovingly of His own chalice.

Great privations had to be borne in her home life also, for it seemed that God's way was to keep her in continual want. After a while her earnings were scarcely sufficient to give her children bread, but in all these anxieties she betook herself to prayer, and in a miraculous way help came from those who were often perfectly unknown to her.

Upon one occasion, when her distress was very great, Anna Maria went to the church of S. Paul, and as she prayed there before a crucifix, she heard a heavenly voice say, "Go home—you will find providence there." Scarcely had she entered her dwelling before a letter came containing money, from one who had never heard from her of the state of mind she was in.

As a wife and mother this holy woman was faithful in discharging every duty, yielding to her husband with much humility, and by her sweetness and patience winning him to a more Christian life than he had before pursued. She brought up her children with the greatest care, not only teaching them what was right, but setting it before them by her own practice, and removing from them every occasion of sin as far as lay in her power. The morning began with prayers, after which the elder ones were sent to work and the younger to school; in the evening she recited with them the rosary and night prayers, and always took care to see that they avoided evil company. On holidays of obligation she was not satisfied with their attendance at Mass alone, but sent them also to Catechism, or to hear some preacher, and thus she neglected nothing which was a means of grounding them in the knowledge of their religious duties, praying always that they might each receive grace to practise at home and abroad what they learned, and become faithful children of Christ's Church.

The charity of this poor woman was extended to all who might need it. Wonderful conversions were granted to her prayers, and while her first thought was for the souls of others, she did not forget to aid them in temporal trials. Though so poor, she would share what she had with those who were still poorer, and if she had nothing to give she would then try and interest some richer person in their favour. Her visits to the hospitals were frequent, and she would sometimes take her daughters with her, hoping to teach them great charity for the sufferers.

Anna Maria did not escape those calumnies and injuries which in some degree are always the portion of those whom God loves best. One person, a neighbour, conceived a violent hatred for her, which lasted more than eight years, during which time she accused her both in public and private of being a hypocrite, and of leading a most wicked life, although trying to disguise it under the appearance of piety; yet during this long trial the servant of God only prayed for the unhappy woman, and never lost patience or omitted showing her a kindness if ever the opportunity came.

While God thus suffered Madame Taigi to bear trials of so many kinds from His hands, He also led her to practise many severe mortifications by fasting, and especially in abstinence with regard to drinking, for she frequently deprived herself of even a drop of water for a whole week. Wednesday, Friday, and Saturday were days upon which she always fasted, and for special reasons she would undertake special fasts for long periods.

Such a life of fidelity, humility, and penance drew down from heaven the choicest blessings which God gives to souls that are very dear to Him, and she was made the instrument of help and salvation to many. One of the noble families of Rome owed to her prayers the restoration to health of many of their children, who had before been constantly ailing. One day she was making the pilgrimage of the Seven Churches with some friends, when a drenching rain compelled her to seek shelter in some house near by. There lay a woman dying, the last Sacraments had been administered to her, her friends knelt weeping round her bed, and Anna Maria began to pray, making over the sick person the sign of the Cross with a small picture of the Blessed Virgin. Presently the rain ceased, and she left the room, to continue her pilgrimage, but before she had descended the stairs, the watchers by the sick-bed ran to tell her that the dying woman was restored, and had begun to speak once more.

Amidst all these graces she showed the greatest humility, never speaking of spiritual helps which she received excepting to her confessor, or by his desire to a few whom she assisted in devoting themselves to the service of God; and in such cases her words were those of a person who feels herself completely unworthy of the gifts of her Divine Spouse.

At last, Anna Maria became so ill and suffering that she was forced to keep her bed, and for more than nine months she lay there, bearing acute pain with perfect sweetness and submission, her one consolation being that she received Holy Communion daily.

In the month of June, 1837, she was seized with fever, but it passed, and no one felt any special anxiety as to her state, yet she herself knew that death was near, and so she began gradually to set all her household affairs in order, that she might have nothing to occupy her but heavenly things.

Towards the last, Anna Maria called her husband and children to her, to take leave of them, placing them first under the special protection of the Blessed Virgin, and then of S. Philomena, to whom she had ever a great devotion; and after receiving the last Sacraments her sufferings increased, and she lost the power of speech, but it was God's Will that she should expire almost suddenly — when those who had watched her thought she would live some hours—upon a Friday night, as she had herself predicted.

Anna Maria's extraordinary graces and virtues had not—with all her efforts—been hidden from the world, and when she was dead, visitors came from distant parts to kneel beside her tomb; and so many persons have given testimony of the sanctity of this poor woman, that it is believed God will so make manifest the gifts He bestowed upon her as to lead to her being raised to the altars of the Church. Meanwhile, the history of her humble life is given as an example of piety and devotion, that we who read it may seek grace to give ourselves wholly to God, as she did, and while dwelling in the world, meeting its trials and difficulties, struggling perhaps against its temptations, and burdened with its cares, may, like Anna Maria Taigi, learn to find God in all things, and keep closely united to Him.

Anne Catherine Emmerich.

AWAY in the little Westphalian village of Coesfeld there dwelt, about a hundred years ago, a sweet, bright, loving child, who was dear to all who knew her, and dearer still to God because of her innocent and guileless heart, which was given entirely to Him. She was not among those who are great in the world: her home was a miserable hut roofed over with moss-grown thatch, while inside there were but a few broken chairs, a table, and a spinning-wheel, for furniture, with hay and straw to serve as beds. But Jesus lay in the stable of Bethlehem, and many of His dearest saints have been born and reared in poverty and want, and little Anne Catherine Emmerich learned in that humble cottage to live and suffer, and at last die in the love and fear of God.

The child's parents were honest, hard-working, and pious people, and she would often say that her earliest recollection was being taught the " Our Father," and having her tiny fingers bent to trace the form of the cross upon her brow and upon her breast. When she sent little Catherine to play, the good mother would tell her that the holy angels, and even the Child Jesus, came to join in the games of those children who were pure and gentle, and the little thing, in her innocence, took these words in their literal meaning, and would often stand gazing up at the sky, longing to see the heavenly visitors appear. She was taught also to say short prayers as she went to or from church, and in after years she has said that she accustomed herself to make the cross on her brow and lips and heart, which should be so many keys to lock out all wicked thoughts or words.

Little Anne Catherine had to work hard every day, for her parents trained her with some austerity, believing it the way to prepare her for the steep rough road of the cross when she was older. As quite a small child she had to go to the field at break of day in summer and winter time, to fetch up the horse, which was a vicious creature, and often more than a man could manage, although with Anne Catherine it was always gentle. She had also to tend the cows, to carry wood, and to help in the hard work of harvesting when she was but five or six years old.

The child had much to suffer, for though her parents were constantly thanking God for the graces He had given her soul, they were so afraid of her feeling any pride or complacency in herself, that they concealed their joy and satisfaction under a harsh manner, punishing her with severity for the smallest fault.

But the little peasant girl was happy in her hard life—happy because she was always conscious of the Presence of God; and while she prayed to Him in the fields, with her cows grazing around her, her heart was filled with love and the desire to please Him. In a corner of the poor cottage there hung its one ornament — a little picture of the Blessed Virgin with the Holy Child in her arms — and this was an altar for Anne Catherine, where she often prayed, and where, as almost a baby, she would lay her favourite toys, and any little gifts she might receive, as an offering to the Infant Jesus.

When any of these things disappeared she was delighted, because she believed it a sign that the Divine Child was pleased with the little sacrifice she had made for Him. The fear of offending God was so strong, that even at three years of age the child was often heard to pray for and desire death, so as to avoid sinning as she grew older. But the Divine purpose in bringing little Anne Catherine Emmerich into the world was an unusual one. Instead of dying early, as in her simplicity she desired, instead of growing up to do some great work for His glory in the world, she was to be a perpetual and willing sacrifice, offering herself to God for the sins of others, bearing their pains, and learning in suffering strange secrets concerning Christ and His Church. All this was to be the work of the untaught, humble peasant girl — the work of standing as a victim before the Almighty for His sinful creatures, offering, in union with our blessed Lord, her tears, her pains, her prayers, in expiation of their sins.

As a very little thing, she would ask God to send upon her the illness under which she saw some other child suffering, and often her prayers were granted at once. If she saw one of her companions commit a fault, she would directly lay upon herself some penance; and if she was asked what made her do this, she would say that God made her feel that desire in her heart, and she could not help it. One time Anne Catherine's mother was ill in bed with erysipelas, and her face was terribly swollen, but at the prayer of the child the pain and the swelling passed to her own head, and as she suffered, her mother became suddenly quite well.

At four years old this brave little girl began to practise rising in the night for prayer, going out to a field on the hill above her father's cottage, and kneeling there for two or three hours, and often even to the dawn of day. We must not think this was easy to Anne Catherine Emmerich—she was like other children of her age, and felt weary and sleepy after her day's hard toil; she dreaded, too, going alone into the darkness, but because it was God's Will that she should do this, He allowed her to hear the voice of her angel bidding her rise and pray, and she obeyed directly, though tears would spring to her eyes at the effort it cost her.

Many children much older than this little peasant girl would find much prayer very difficult, and would hardly know any subjects to occupy them for so long a time; but to her the hours went fast because she had so much to ask for others, and as God intended her to be useful to the souls of many who were sinning against Him, she was allowed to see, like a picture in her mind, all sorts of scenes in distant places. Sometimes it would be a soul in its death-agony, unrepentant and passing from the world without confessing its sins; sometimes it would be the sight of some poor homeless child, or the miseries of prisoners and captives, or a traveller in danger of perishing. Such were the visions which were sent to little Anne Catherine from God, to awaken her pity and her fervent prayers and penance.

But the greater number of her petitions were for the holy souls, and often during the winter nights she would kneel upon the frozen snow, or in summer scourge herself with sharp nettles, that so she might get them relief. As quite a young child, she also was permitted to see in vision the scenes which are contained in the Old Testament history, and many a night when her father was resting in his arm-chair by the cottage fire after a hard day's toil, little Anne Catherine would sit on his knee, describing these things to him so wonderfully, that he would exclaim, "Child, who told thee this?" and she could only answer, "Oh, father, I seem to see it all quite plainly."

Jesus not only taught this little girl these wonderful things, but He also showed Himself to her in her common daily life.

When she was working in the fields, or driving home her cows, He would come to her side in the form of a little boy, and help her, telling her all about His own childhood, and the humiliations and sufferings He had to undergo. At other times He would appear before her in the form of a child bearing a heavy cross, and the expression of weariness, yet patience, in His eyes, touched the heart of little Anne Catherine with such sorrow and such love, that she too would seize upon the heaviest piece of wood she could find, and carry it on her shoulders as long as her strength lasted, so that she might imitate Jesus.

This wonderful intercourse of our dear Lord had a great influence upon this little peasant girl's heart. Seeing Him so frequently in vision, she never lost the recollection of His blessed Presence, and so in her games with other children she always managed to put in some thought of spiritual things. Sometimes she would persuade them to form a little procession as they went along the lanes between the thick hedgerows, imagining themselves in the company of the angels; again, she would model in sand the holy places of Jerusalem of which God had taught her, the hill of Calvary or the garden of Gethsemane.

At about seven years old Anne Catherine prepared to make her first confession, and she was so filled with contrition for the faults of her little life, which she imagined must be mortal sins, that she burst into a flood of tears when she knelt before the priest, in her fear that he would refuse her absolution, on account of such great offences against God. Four years after, she made her First Communion, and then her one thought was to put herself entirely into God's hands, for Him to do with her what was His Will. As she went to the church upon that happy day, she kept her eyes shut all the way, lest she should see anything that might even for a second turn her mind from God. Her request was then that she "might be made a good child," and the prayer must have found favour with the Almighty, for that First Communion day seems to be a fresh starting-point upon the path of holiness for Anne Catherine, as from that time her humility and sweetness and mortification seemed to have still deeper root. But though God gave her so many divine favours, He did not spare her from being exposed to the attacks of the evil one. At night, when she and her eldest brother would get up and kneel on the floor, praying with outstretched arms, a terrible voice which made them tremble would order them back to bed, but though the boy obeyed, Anne Catherine prayed on until the tempter left her in peace.

When she went across the narrow path to the old cross on the hill for her midnight prayer, the child often would see a horrible monster standing before her, but the sign of the cross either drove it away, or prevented it touching her.

Once, on her way to church, in the dusky light of early morning, a form something like a dog rushed past, striking her face so roughly that it swelled to a great size, and was only cured by holy water. Thus, and in many other ways was Anne Catherine assaulted by her spiritual enemy, but God's angel preserved her from every snare.

After such a childhood, it is not strange that as she grew older this girl should have a great longing to advance in the service of God, and a hope that He would put clearly before her the life which should assist her to follow Him more closely. Long before, she had made a vow to her Divine Spouse to enter into a convent when she was old enough; and though she had never seen the exact way in which she could do this, her confidence in God was so strong, that she never doubted but that He would make it possible. However, at twelve years of age Anne Catherine was sent out as a servant to a farmer's wife, who says she was a "quiet, gentle little girl;" but when they laughed at her thought of being some day a nun, she would beg them not to talk like that, for it would be so after a while. After three years had been spent thus, the girl's father and mother took her home to assist in field work, and then when the bell of the convent at Coesfeld rang for Vespers or the Angelus, such a longing filled her heart, that she knew not how to bear it, and a voice seemed borne to her upon the wind, which said, "Go into a convent, let be what may."

Anne Catherine grew very sad, so that her

mother asked why it was, and when she heard of this desire, she was very angry, and said how absurd it was to expect that a poor sickly peasant child could ever be a nun. But the girl always answered, "God is infinitely rich, and He will bring it about for me;" and with this thought she waited in hope and confidence. The next thing her mother did was to apprentice her to a dressmaker, and thus she spent two years of her life, keeping her heart in union with God as she plied her needle, and seeing many a fair vision of Jesus, His Mother, and the Saints, as she accomplished difficult pieces of work.

After two years, illness overtook Anne Catherine, so that she returned to her home, and upon her recovery she began to go out daily to needlework, in the hope of gaining enough to take as a dower into some convent. But the little money she earned was spent as soon as she had it, for the poor, whom she so much loved. Strongly as she desired the life of a Religious, her compassion for the needy was stronger still, and she sacrificed her great longing for their sake. It was a hard time just then, for parents and brothers and sisters opposed her plans, and she herself was distressed by a fear lest she was growing cold in God's service. Happily in all this desolation and darkness an opportunity came for her to receive the Sacrament of Confirmation, and a wonderful strength of heart was given to her then, which helped her to accept with increased sweetness all the blame and unkind treatment offered her, and also to lay upon herself fresh practices of penance in expiation for the guilt of others. This peasant girl had always been frequent in practising the Devotion of the Stations of the Cross, which were erected at intervals along the steep path which led up the hill from Coesfeld; and now that her days were busy with work, she made the Stations at night, when to reach them she must climb over the crumbling walls, and grope through a dense gloomy wood, because the city gates were shut. At length, after long delay and bitter disappointments and humiliations, the peasant maiden was received into a convent of the Augustinian order at Dulmen, by the influence of a friend who was going there herself; and so Anne Catherine took leave of her parents and her humble cottage home. Though so very poor in earthly goods, this holy girl was wonderfully rich in heavenly graces; but in order to sanctify her soul more, God blinded the eyes of the nuns to her great perfection, so that it seemed to them as if she was full of faults. Her life there was a difficult one. Nobody liked her, and she expected from day to day to be sent home, and all her meekness and patience failed to overcome the strong dislike and distrust of the community; and yet God's power was so great that He carried her through all these obstacles, so that the time came for her to kneel before the altar and make her final vows of religion. Upon that profession-day Anne Catherine's face glowed with such a heavenly sweetness, that for once the sisters felt drawn lovingly towards her, but this affection was but passing—it was not God's way of perfecting her. At the close of the year 1811 this convent was suppressed, the church closed, and the community had to arrange for their departure. Although she had suffered so much within those walls, Anne Catherine was greatly troubled at leaving the place where she had bound herself irrevocably to God; and, becoming very ill, she stayed on alone till spring in her little damp cell, where the birds paid friendly visits to her, and even the mice seemed welcome in her solitude. One old servant and the abbé who had belonged to the convent had pity upon the poor deserted nun, and provided her with what food they could obtain, and in spring they took her to the house of a widow woman in Dulmen, where she could have a room. Before one day had been passed there Anne Catherine was taken dangerously ill, soon becoming too weak to rise from her bed. This went on till autumn, when, after receiving the last Sacraments, she grew slightly better, so that she could be removed into another lodging, which had a little garden opening from it.

Here her wonderful visions became more frequent, more marvellous. Our Lord, who had imprinted in her heart so long the love of the cross, saw fit to let her bear its mark upon her poor weak body, and to be one of those whom He has chosen to bear His own sacred wounds in hands and feet and side, from which drops of blood were seen to flow. Many doubted, many were angry, some suspicious, some puzzled, and yet it was a truth that there, in the little village of Dulmen, the lowly, despised Sister Emmerich was lying with the sacred stigma of the Passion of Christ. That strange grace was the beginning of a sort of long and weary martyrdom. She who had loved silence and solitude was now a public character, one who for years must bear a course of visits for questioning and examination; one who should be deemed an impostor, and mistrusted by even the priests of God. Larger books give the history of this time, but ours is rather a story of her early days as a little peasant maiden, and we can but glance at the closing years of her life. If those years were trying, they were filled with the richest of God's graces. If Jesus brought her the cross, He brought her, too, the love and strength with which to bear it; and He led her in vision through every scene of His most sacred Passion, so that she might patiently endure all suffering for Him. In her own account of the "Dolorous Passion of Christ" we shall see how she went step by step from Gethsemane to Calvary in a series of visions granted by God for her comfort and sanctification, and also for the instruction of the entire Catholic world; and then when suffering had done its perfect work, and every grace the Holy Sacraments can give was granted her, Anne Catherine peacefully kissed her crucifix, and lovingly exclaiming, "Help me, help me, Lord Jesus!" passed into the valley of the shadow of death — that death which was the happy ending of life's sorrows and pains.

This was on the evening of the 9th of February, 1824. On the 13th she was carried to the grave, with the whole population of Dulmen following her to the quiet corner in the parish churchyard which had been chosen for her resting-place.

Although Sister Emmerich has neither been pronounced "saint" or "blessed" by the voice of the Church, it seems that she merits a place among those whose virtues have, by God's Will, been made more publicly known, for it is a history of simple love and fidelity to her Lord, from which all may draw help and example. Even if she should never in future years be raised to the altars of the Church on earth, we may be sure that her place in heaven is very near to Him whom she set before her as a pattern of suffering and sacrifice, and her crown set with many a gem gained amidst the hardships of her child life, the humiliations of the convent, or the mysterious agonies of her later years.

Curé d'Ars.

IN the summer days of 1859 a holy life was drawing to its close in the midst of the laborious duties of the priesthood. Toils, vigils, fastings had worn the weak frame of M. Vianney, the much-loved Curé of Ars, almost to a shadow, and yet he struggled against the feebleness which gained upon him, and performed his usual duties in the crowded heated church until within a few days of the hour when his long course of charity and sacrifice was ended.

His was truly a life all given to God: the first sweet days of childhood, the strength and earnest purpose of his youth, were consecrated to the one great end—the service of his

Creator; and then in manhood the promise of earlier years was fulfilled in his priesthood, in which his whole heart was given in the highest and most perfect way to the work he had undertaken for the glory of God.

He was born at Dardilly, a small village not far from Lyons, in a humble farmhouse which had been the dwelling-place of the Vianneys for several generations, and where many a poor wanderer had received food and shelter for the love of God.

Before his birth, his pious mother had often begged of God to accept her little child for His special service, and upon the same day that he came into the world he received in baptism the names of Jean Baptiste and of Marie.

Mme. Vianney watched over her little son with the greatest care, turning his earliest thoughts to God and the Blessed Virgin, and teaching him the meaning of his special consecration to them.

With the first dawn of reason there appeared

signs of wonderful beauty of soul in the little Jean-Marie. At three years old he would go into retired corners to pray, and kneel down at morning and midday to recite the angelus his mother taught him. The first gift he received from her was a tiny statue of the Blessed Virgin, and this he prized as a great treasure, never parting with it by day, and keeping it beside him on his little bed when he went to sleep. If any pain or trouble made him cry, Jean-Marie was at once consoled with an image or a rosary, and he tells us that his first sacrifice — to a little child, a great one — was giving up a small rosary to his sister because she had taken a fancy to it.

The child's remarkable piety grew with his growth, and the simple villagers would say to his parents, when they noticed his devotion at Holy Mass, "You must certainly make your little son a priest."

When Jean-Marie was about eight years old, a great storm of infidelity swept over his native land; its sanctuaries were profaned and deserted; the Holy Sacrifice could only be offered in fear and secrecy by some priest who thus imperilled his own life and the lives of the few faithful worshippers who gathered together; and, like many another village, Dardilly saw its little church closed and its bell silent.

But in the boy's heart his faith was firmly rooted, and though he could no longer kneel with his mother in the presence of the Blessed Sacrament, he would pray to God in his heart, or seek some corner in the quiet woods where he might put his dear image of Mary in the hollow trunk of a tree, and, kneeling down, ask for mercy upon unhappy France.

Jean-Marie was now thought old enough to lead his father's cows and the few sheep he possessed to the pastures, some distance from the little farm; and so, with his staff in one hand, and his small image of the Virgin clasped to his breast, he would take his way, and get the other shepherd boys sometimes to kneel down and say an Ave with him.

The Vianneys had always practised hospitality to the poor and homeless, and the beggars who went to the farmhouse were sure of a welcome, and a share of the hot potatoes which were served up for the children's supper, before they were shown to their sleeping-places in the barn or cellar. Jean-Marie, too, brought in all the poor he could find, and would beg from his mother some article of clothing for them, for his childish heart seemed already filled with that boundless charity which burned so brightly through the after-course of his life.

When he was with children of his own age he tried to teach them something about God, beginning with the Pater noster and Ave, and the acts of Faith, Hope, and Charity.

By the time this little boy was eleven years of age, the violence of the haters of religion seemed partly abating, and as a few banished priests had returned, there was now an opportunity for Jean-Marie to prepare for his first confession. But the times were still dangerous, and great secrecy was necessary to be observed in all religious worship, so that no exact information remains as to the time of the boy's First Communion, but it is supposed to have been in the year 1799.

Many records are left us of the purity and sweetness of Jean-Marie's life in his family. He was always obedient, and thus set an unfailing example to his brothers and sisters; always industrious in his work of tilling and sowing his father's fields; always praying in his heart to God while his hands were busy.

At the time of his First Communion, Jean-Marie spoke to his parents of his longing to become a priest, but in those days of persecution such a hope seemed vain. However, after the storm came the time when the churches of France were re-opened, and priests once more publicly offered the Holy Sacrifice, and Jean-Marie ventured to disclose his long-cherished aim to the Curé of Ecully, who gave him great encouragement.

The one difficulty was that his education

had been entirely neglected. Other boys of his age were advanced in studies of which he knew nothing, and poor Jean-Marie had to struggle against the disadvantages of a bad memory and a very slow conception, so that he was often quite discouraged.

Yet he persevered bravely, in spite of his dulness, until a sudden inspiration led him to make a vow to go on foot to the tomb of S. John Francis Regis, to ask the gift of sufficient learning to become a good servant of God. His prayer was not in vain, for he obtained so great a measure of the grace he had sought, as to astonish both his master and his companions.

Jean-Marie now lived with his relations at Ecully, and there he tried to carry on his old practice of feeding the homeless poor, as he had done at Dardilly. Once meeting a man with no shoes, he took off his own and gave them to him, arriving at his home barefoot, to the vexation of his father.

A great trouble came to the young Vianney

in the year 1809. He had just reached the age when he was liable to be called to the military service, and an order was sent for him to join the troops at Bayonne, to the great distress of his family.

Another young man was found to act in his place, but at the last moment he changed his mind and returned the money which had been paid him, and this disappointment brought a severe illness upon Jean-Marie, so that by the order of the authorities he was obliged to be sent to the hospital instead of going at once to Bayonne. While there he talked much to his relations who went to see him of the holy Will of God, and seemed quite able to accept at His hands a life so different from his choice, if such was best. But it was the purpose of the Almighty to deliver him after he had been tried, and his deliverance was brought about strangely. The day had come when the departure of his troop was fixed, and Jean-Marie offered no complaint or resistance, but he went to pray in a church, and so completely forgot the time, that he let the hour pass by when he had to present himself. When he did appear, the recruiting officer threatened to send him in chains to Bayonne, but others interposed on his behalf, so that he was allowed to go quietly on his way with a sad heart, because he had such a great repugnance to the soldier's life which seemed before him. As a comfort under these troubled thoughts, he took out his rosary, that prayer to his heavenly Mother might beguile the way. As he went along, a stranger came up with him, and asked where he was going, and Jean-Marie told his story; upon which the young man bade him follow him, and at the same time took up his heavy knapsack, which after his illness he could scarcely carry along. Thus they travelled all day, following quiet and unfrequented paths, until at night they reached the door of a lonely house, at which the stranger knocked. Upon a voice answering from within, the unknown guide explained to the man and woman who dwelt there that their hospitality was needed for the night, and Jean-Marie was admitted, but the stranger vanished, and was never again heard of by him whom he had so greatly befriended.

When morning came the master of the house offered to show him a place where he should be perfectly safe, and conducted him to the village of Noës, where the Maire took him under his protection, and found him a lodging in the house of the Mère Fayot. In this village he opened a little school, where he laboured from morning till night in instructing the children of that part, and when the summer took his pupils to field-work, Jean-Marie found other means of employment.

For some time he maintained himself thus, beloved by all who knew him, but in the year 1810 his younger brother offered to fill his place as a soldier; and as he was accepted, Jean-Marie had no longer any motive for concealing himself, and therefore returned to his home and resumed his studies under the Curé of Ecully.

It was upon the 9th of August, 1815, that M. Vianney was ordained priest when he had reached the age of twenty-nine years, and he was appointed vicar to his much-beloved master, M. Balley, until about two years later, when he was made Curé of Ars.

We hear that when he first caught sight of the roofs of his parish, he knelt down to implore a blessing upon the people committed to his care. From the beginning of his life there he chose the church as his chief dwelling-place, going there at daybreak, and remaining until the evening angelus. Did any one want him, it was in the church he was found, and he made so little use of the presbytery, that it wore a strange forlorn look, as of a place deserted by its owner.

The village of Ars at the time of M. Vianney's arrival was destitute of holiness and piety, the young people were giddy and trifling, the old careless, and Sunday was a time for meetings in the tavern or dancing on the green.

The Curé won his people by the force of love, by his prayers, and the Holy Sacrifice. Fortunately he had just a few faithful souls to aid his labours, and one of the most powerful of these was Mdlle. d'Ars, the lady of the castle, whose time was divided between prayer, visits to the poor, and the care of her household. The first means he found of reforming his parish was establishing in his church the perpetual adoration of the Blessed Sacrament, finding the adorers at first in the pious lady of Ars, a good old labouring man, who loved to leave his pickaxe and spade and hoe at the door, while he knelt for hours before the tabernacle after returning from work, and a poor widow who managed the Curé's household. Just then a person very much respected for her piety, named Mdlle. Pignaaut, came from Lyons to the village. and with her the holy priest completed his little company, who two by two would kneel in the church, one in the sanctuary and one in the chapel of Our Lady, so that Jesus was no longer left alone.

Another aim always before the Curé was to bring his people to a more frequent use of the Sacraments, and after a little while this great desire was granted, and a spirit of devotion spread amongst them; the pleasures of the tavern and the dancing gave way before his prayers, and worshippers flocked to the Mass, to Vespers, Compline, and the Rosary.

The next work of this zealous pastor was to restore and ornament his church, for dearly as he loved poverty in his personal life, he was profuse in what he gave for the beautifying of the temple of God. He built several small chapels, for the purpose of enlarging the space as well as to cultivate the devotion of his people. The first of these he dedicated to his own patron, S. John the Baptist, and the second to S. Philomena, to whom he had always a marked devotion.

After working with much success among these people for five years, M. Vianney was thought by his superiors more fitted for a place where his great zeal for souls might have a wider range, and he was accordingly appointed Curé of Salles. But it was evidently God's Will that he should remain with the villagers of Ars, for twice over his little stock of furniture was packed, but the overflowing of the Seine rendered the journey impossible; and during this delay his people addressed such an earnest appeal to the Vicar-general, that he was persuaded to leave them their much-loved Curé to watch over them.

When M. Vianney wished to obtain some special graces for himself or his people, or when he wished to make reparation for some great offence which had been offered to God, he would often pass several days without taking any food whatever, and at other times he lived upon the poorest diet, frequently having but black bread and boiled potatoes. His people often brought him some little tempting dish, beseeching him to eat it, but it was certain to find its way to a beggar's wallet or to one of the poor villagers.

One day, the good Soeur Lacon, who was his housekeeper after the death of the widow Renard, made a beautiful pie for the Curé, which she placed in an old cupboard in the kitchen of the presbytery, and impatiently waited for M. Vianney to return in the evening. When he came in, she hurried to him and asked him to have a little piece of pie.

"I should like it very much," he said, to her great delight, and she flew to the cupboard. Alas! no pie was to be found, and, suspecting the Curé had discovered it, she went back in the greatest indignation.

"Monsieur, this is really too bad—I did not give the pie to you, it was my own."

"Why then did you put it in the presbytery?" he answered, quietly. "I thought I had a right to dispose of what I find in my own house."

Another time the good woman had prepared a dish of a small thin cake eaten in that part of France, called "matefaims." M. Vianney had watched her as she mixed her flour, and when all was finished, and the dish placed before him, he joined his hands and raised his eyes to heaven; but while the others were making the sign of the cross, he jumped up, and seizing the dish, ran down with it to the door, where he gave the contents to some of the poor who were lingering about. In this way the Curé of Ars practised both charity and mortification, and it seemed impossible to satisfy his thirst for suffering. He would pull out the straw from his palliasse, and thus make his hard bed still harder; then he discarded it altogether, and taking a stone for his pillow, slept on the floor of the granary; and thus through sufferings inflicted on himself, through sufferings permitted or sent from the hand of God, he passed onward and upward, till he became conformed to the likeness of his Master. Horrible visitations of the evil one were allowed to try him for a long course of years, until he became so accustomed to them, that he would sleep peacefully amidst noise and disturbance which aroused others. Evil was spoken of him by men, but he welcomed these trials as a means of self-humiliation, and believed that contempt was what he justly merited, rather than the love and veneration of the great mass of people who crowded to his confessional, from the knowledge of his sanctity. But none of these things disturbed the peace of his soul, and at a later period of his life he would speak of this time of strife and suffering as happy days, in which God granted him his most earnest desires.

In the year 1825, M. Vianney had founded a home for friendless or orphan girls, called "The Providence," beginning, in a house bought for the purpose, with two young persons whom he had trained himself to manage it. All the property these two had to take with them was a pot of butter and some dry cheeses (and these even were the gifts of a charitable lady), excepting their beds and a few necessary articles for household use. In a few days a widow woman of the village and another joined them, and a free school was first opened for the little girls of the parish, but very soon children from a greater distance were taken in, and the number quickly increased. Thus was established the "Providence of Ars," but many difficulties arose from which God always delivered them. One day there was no flour, the village did not contain a baker, and there were eighty children to feed. One of the mistresses said that Jeanne, who made the bread, must bake the handful of flour still left, and then they must wait for more. She went to tell the Curé. "Put your leaven into the little bit of flour you have, and bake as usual to-morrow," he said.

Jeanne obeyed, and the next day she tells that the dough kept rising under her fingers, and it swelled and thickened, until from that morsel of flour she made ten large loaves of more than twenty pounds weight each. Thus God showed that the house and all in it was especially under His Divine protection.

With his constant daily labour for souls, his austere life, his short nightly rest, and long hours in the confessional, the prolonged existence of M. Vianney seemed a continual miracle, but in the year 1843 a severe illness seemed likely to prove fatal. The malady gained ground so rapidly that it was judged well to administer the last Sacraments. The whole village was praying for their friend and Father, but a Mass was offered for his recovery at the altar of S. Philomena, and at the very time he fell into a calm sleep, which was the beginning of his recovery, and for many a year after that he continued his labours among his people. There were times when he strove to leave them, that he might find a more solitary life, where, as he said, he might weep over his sins and prepare for death; but though he had even started on his way, the entreaties of those who pursued him brought him back, for God seemed to deny him that tranquil ending of life for which he longed, and chose for him to die at his post, as a soldier and servant of the Cross.

And so at length, after his long years of toil, the news was told from one to another of the villagers of Ars that their Curé was dead. He had blessed them for the last time, and the poor emaciated body was lying in the presbytery, where pilgrims came from every part of France to weep and pray around him. More than three hundred priests and six thousand people took part in the funeral procession, and listened to the address of the Bishop of Belley, who told before his coffin the history of the life and death of the venerable man — told not so much the secrets of the wondrous mystical union between God and the pure soul of His servant, as the secret of his sanctity, which lay in the fidelity to grace, the generous loving service of his God throughout the whole course of his long life.

In the history of the Curé d'Ars we see the power of the Holy Spirit triumphing over the absence of great natural gifts. The brilliant intellect, the profound learning, the polish of education and high breeding were not his, but the sweetness of his charity towards God and man shone in his look and tone, and won souls from sin; and the poor simple country curé, whose prayers and penances, instructions and labours, were all acts performed for the sole honour and glory of God, is now venerated by the whole Catholic Church as one more of the holy humble followers of Christ whom they hope to see among the list of the Saints, to be invoked by all who need their prayers as they struggle with the world's temptations and difficulties.

"How sweet to die when we have lived on the Cross," was one of the sayings of the holy Curé of Ars. Let us ask some faint reflection of his love of suffering, so that we too may lay up a treasure for the hour of death, and find that way of the Cross our way to heaven.

Marie Eustelle Harpain.

ONE June day in the year 1842, a visitor to the little French village of Saint-Pallais would have noticed the grief which prevailed among the humble peasantry dwelling there, and would have seen them gathered in knots of two or three, talking together of one whose virtues had made her deeply loved and venerated; one who, as they all believed, had passed from earth, to dwell for ever in the presence of God.

She had left behind her no property, no things of value; and yet her rosary, her few books of devotion, even scraps of paper bearing her handwriting, were being eagerly seized upon as memorials of the saintly

Marie Eustelle Harpain, the sempstress of Saint-Pallais, whose simple life had been given to the love and worship of Jesus in the Blessed Sacrament, to the one absorbing purpose of awakening a burning devotion to the Most Holy Eucharist in the hearts of her countrymen and women.

She never guessed, in her sweet humility, that God had chosen her, a poor weak woman, as the instrument, in His hands, of kindling a flame of love to the Blessed Sacrament in the hearts of thousands; that her lips were to utter the first notes of praise which others should take up, and swell into the chorus of adoration which has become the marked devotion of our own days. All that Marie Eustelle aspired to was that she might live and die for Jesus, that she might see Him worthily loved in His Sacramental Presence.

Her parents, René Harpain and Marie Picotin, belonged to a humble class of life, but the father appears to have been one of those who are satisfied in fulfilling, or partly fulfilling, the obligations of a Catholic, but who felt neither love nor generosity towards the God Who had created him. Happily the little child had a good and pious mother, who taught her to say the Our Father and Hail Mary as soon as she could speak, and who watched over her innocent soul with the greatest care.

Marie Eustelle seems to have been a lively little girl, intelligent, and very affectionate, and with an intense fondness for pleasure. She quickly learned to read, and the New Testament and the Imitation were her first books, yet she lighted upon some of those bad songs which are like poison to the minds of so many poor children; and but for her openness in showing what she had found to her mother, perhaps the seeds of evil might have been sown in the heart of the little Eustelle.

She was sent to school at six years of age, although her parents could ill afford the payment. But here the child's intelligence and amiability won her such praise and favour, that she became vain; and this appearing in her conduct at home, alarmed her mother, and caused her to beg the mistress not to flatter Eustelle, or give her any chance of display. But it was not easy for her teacher to help loving and making much of the child, who was so sweet, so caressing, and who won the hearts of all her companions by her pretty engaging ways; and when Marie Eustelle was taken from school at ten years of age, she had grown proud and self-complacent—faults over which she bitterly mourned in later days.

Her remarkable skill in needlework had already shown itself, and as French children of the poorer classes early begin to earn their daily bread, Eustelle's mother thought of apprenticing her to some seamstress, that she might learn sufficient to make her independent. But as to do this it would be necessary to send her from home, this good woman was anxious that her child should make her First Communion before she went out into the dangerous temptations of the world; so, until she was sufficiently prepared for this great grace, Marie Eustelle was to remain with her parents, and busy herself in all the little duties of the household which were fit for her.

Up to this time there had been no special sign of God's favour, no great longing after holiness, but it seemed as if it was the Divine purpose that the Blessed Sacrament, which was to be the one great attraction of her after life, should be the means of first rousing the child's heart to sorrow and to love. As soon as she heard that she might prepare for First Communion, she almost ceased from the play and pleasure she had loved so much; she began to pay great attention to her prayers, and a reserve and gentleness appeared in her manner, which was new to her. The child was resolved to avoid everything which might in the smallest way hinder her from receiving all the grace which she knew Jesus was ready to bestow. Many a little act of self-denial was practised then which she had never thought of before, and she chose to go through the devotion of the Way of the Cross four times every week, with the intention of obtaining grace to make a good First Communion.

It was on the Feast of Corpus Christi that Jesus first rested in the heart of Marie Eustelle—the young heart which still understood His love so little, and yet was so full of happiness and earnest resolves. The further grace of Confirmation was granted her upon the same day, and thus the child was strengthened to meet the attractions of the world, of which as yet she knew nothing.

For some little time Eustelle practised her good resolutions, and she found help in frequent visits to a company of religious women who had consecrated their lives to God, and whose especial object was to visit the sick in hospitals, and teach girls of the peasant class.

On Sundays, after assisting at Mass and at Vespers in her parish church, Eustelle would hasten to the house of these good sisters, who welcomed her so kindly; and sometimes she would dream happily of a future time when perhaps God might call her to that same service, dreams which were not destined to become realities, because of the far different vocation which was hers.

At fourteen years old Marie Eustelle was apprenticed to a needlewoman, with whom she was to remain during the day, returning home at night; and then it was that she became unfaithful to grace in trifling things, and yielded to the vanity and self-love which were in youth her greatest temptations. She was pleasing in her appearance, and her sweet engaging manners won for her the love of all who saw her; and the young girls who were her companions were delighted if Eustelle would share in their amusements. She soon yielded, and became so fond of dress and of dancing, that she has herself said that she counted the hours until the time arrived when she could indulge in this diversion, and her chief thought was how to please and make herself loved and admired. Though she had thus grown cold in devotion and turned away from the service of God, Eustelle still regularly assisted at Mass on Sundays and holydays, she did not omit her prayers or neglect the days of abstinence, but she very rarely approached the Sacraments, being quite content to receive Holy Communion twice only in the year. But was she happy at this time? Ah, no. In spite of her apparent gaiety, her bright smile and merry voice, there was no peace, no rest in her heart; for Jesus her Saviour called her many a time to come to Him and take upon her His light yoke, His happy service, and in quiet moments she would hesitate and waver, wishing it was possible to have God and the world together. At times the Evil One would tempt the girl to despair of salvation, to think that her passions were beyond her strength to conquer. She would even say that

God had not willed to save her, that she was not one of those for whom Christ died on Calvary. Thus was Marie Eustelle resisting her Lord and turning from His loving invitations, when the Lenten time of 1829 approached, and upon the evening of Shrove Tuesday she was dancing merrily at a ball among her usual companions. The clock struck twelve as they sat at the supper-table, and the giddy party did not notice it, but suddenly the thought flashed upon Eustelle that Ash-Wednesday had begun.

"We are eating meat, I shall not go on," she said to the person nearest to her, and she kept bravely to her determination, in spite of all the laughter and raillery of her friends.

Not long after there was a jubilee of fifteen days, and this young girl, feeling herself strongly drawn towards God in that season of special grace, went to confession to a very holy priest. He told her that he felt sure God had special designs in her regard, and begged her to be faithful, requiring her to make a promise to give up her dangerous pleasures. His words deeply impressed Marie Eustelle, and she placed herself under the protection of the Blessed Virgin, saying a rosary each day to obtain the grace of a perfect conversion; and yet, when Lent had passed by, she failed in her promises to God, and was tempted to take part in the parties and dancing which had done her soul such harm. But the sweetness was gone out of these pleasures — God was too good to let Eustelle join in them with the delight she once had felt. On her return home she was so miserable, so full of remorse, that the very amusement she best loved became a source of disgust to her. Again she sought the same confessor, acknowledged her unfaithfulness, and assured him that she would henceforth turn her back upon the world; and when he permitted her the happiness of going to Communion, Jesus put His seal upon her soul, and made her heart captive to His love.

If Eustelle had been all for the world, now

the cry of her soul was, "All for God." With bitter tears she mourned over her forgetfulness of Him, her vanity, her wilfulness; and turning to prayer for help to overcome, Divine grace was poured out so abundantly upon her, that she became a changed being. Her friends were greatly displeased when Eustelle no longer shared in their amusements: she had a good deal to bear from those who had flattered and sought her most, but she had learned that the pleasure of the world is hollow and fleeting, and she never again wished to return to it.

Marie Eustelle always declared that it was the Holy Eucharist which had set her free from the chains of sin—she had realised at last the wondrous sweetness of this Heavenly Food, and from henceforth she could care for nothing else.

Very soon she was permitted to communicate every fortnight, but the interval seemed long, because each Communion created within her a fresh desire for this grace and help.

She strove to give herself more and more to Jesus, so that He might rest in her heart more frequently. Every act of self-denial was made as a preparation for receiving the Blessed Sacrament still oftener, and at length she was permitted to do so every Sunday. Then her soul advanced rapidly in holiness; she burned with desire to fulfil the Divine Will; she rose at four in the morning to walk to church, that she might give the first hours of the day to prayer; she separated herself as much as possible from all creatures, that she might wholly belong to Him who had conquered her with His infinite love.

One day the thought of her beautiful hair crossed her mind, and remembering her former vanity, and fearing the temptation might again beset her, she begged her mother's leave to cut off this great ornament, and delightedly replaced it with a bandeau, in the hope of rendering her appearance less pleasing to creatures.

All this change in Marie Eustelle was observed by the whole neighbourhood. People talked angrily of her because she so openly professed herself at enmity with the world; they pointed at her in the streets with coarse rude jests; they taxed her with being a hypocrite, and declared that she only wanted to gain the good opinion of her confessor. They even ventured to say that every confession and Communion was only a piece of acting; and, indeed, her frequent Communions were the chief cause of all this envy and spite. At last her persecutors carried their complaints to Eustelle's confessor, accusing her of idling away her time, and spending her whole day in church. Her parents heard so much of these complaints that they, too, were vexed with Eustelle; but she bore all these trials patiently and gently, for her Lord was everything to her, and while He loved her, she could bear accusations and reproaches without murmuring, because they made her more like Him who suffered so much for her sake.

But this holy girl had other and far worse trials to endure. God sent her trials in the shape of horrible temptations from the enemy of souls, and she tells us that she was "at first a little frightened;" but being quite certain that He who allowed her to be troubled thus would also give her strength to resist every thought which was wrong, she trusted to His power with the simple confidence which kept her safe.

It was thought by a priest who had the care of her soul during this part of her life that Marie Eustelle was called by God to the religious state; but after a short trial it did not seem as if a convent was the right place for her, so that she returned home, to the great delight of her parents, who had grieved exceedingly in the prospect of separation.

But although she was not to have the privilege and help which belongs specially to those who have received the holy habit of religion, Eustelle was permitted to bind herself irrevocably to God by vows of chastity and poverty, desiring to make an unreserved surrender to Him Who asked her whole heart and life.

When about twenty-three years old she ceased going out daily to work, and set up a little business at home, treating the girls whom she employed with great kindness and consideration, and striving to influence them against those idle amusements which had done her own soul such harm in her early days. She loved, too, all those who were poor, and suffering, and sinful, never turning from any, however great their guilt, but praying and entreating God to touch their hearts with sorrow, and treating such characters with great charity and tenderness. "Love Jesus," she would say to all those with whom she could converse. Her soul burned with such ardent devotion to her Divine Lord, that she would gladly have died, if that could gain Him more love, more homage.

During the last three years of Marie

Eustelle's life many special favours were granted her. She would at times see Jesus in the Sacred Host, as the priest held It between his fingers, or Jesus offering Mass in the person of the priest at the altar, with heavenly spirits attending upon Him.

One Sunday, near the moment of consecration, she felt her soul penetrated with the thought of the grandeur of the Holy Sacrifice, and it seemed that she saw a path of light reaching from heaven down to the altar, bordered by clouds of silvery whiteness, upon which rested multitudes of celestial spirits, who appeared waiting for the great moment when their Lord should come down to offer Himself to the Heavenly Father as a Victim for His creatures. So clear was this sight to Eustelle's soul, that it seemed as if she really gazed upon it with her bodily eyes, while her mind was filled with a sense of her unworthiness of the great love of Him who thus descended upon the altar of sacrifice.

The fruit of all these visions was an increase of love, a deepening humility, and a lively gratitude for favours of which she knew herself to be unworthy.

When the Holy Communion was carried to the sick, Marie Eustelle would follow at a short distance, praying earnestly for those who were about to receive the most Sacred Body of her Lord; and when she was permitted by the priest to go to the house of those to whom Viaticum was to be administered, she received the charge with the greatest delight.

But the days drew on when this devoted woman could no longer follow Jesus to the houses of the sick and dying, for she became so weak that she could not drag herself along the streets, and illness after illness attacked her frail body.

On Easter Tuesday, in the year 1842, she knelt for the last time before the Tabernacle, and acute sufferings began, which were however but slight when compared with the pain of being no more able to visit her Lord in

His temple. But Christ dwelt within her, and in her hours of pain and sickness she was unceasingly absorbed in Him. Upon two days every week the Holy Communion was always brought to her, and then only she seemed conscious of what passed around her—the rest of the time she was waiting eagerly for the visits of her Lord and Love.

Upon the Monday before her death Eustelle was lying silently; at last she exclaimed, "They will not then bring me my Lord to-day."

Her sister reminded her that she had received Communion only the day before, and that not until the Thursday would It again be given her. She made no reply, for her submission to the adorable Will of God would not permit of a spoken regret.

Two days passed, and it was Wednesday, and the Feast of SS. Peter and Paul fell upon that day, so the bells of the church were ringing, and Eustelle, roused by their sweet sound, exclaimed, "My Lord is coming."

Once more her sister reminded her that she must wait till the morrow for her Communion. Eustelle replied, "Oh, I thought it was already Thursday," and at once resumed her silent communing with God. But it seemed that the delay was more than her enfeebled frame could bear, and in a few moments she became agitated, as if with some sharp struggle.

"Pray for me—pray to our Lord for me," she gasped. But the shadow was only for a moment; then a ray from the brightness of heaven seemed to fall upon her, and as she raised her eyes, and murmured the Holy Name, she passed into the enjoyment of the presence of Him who had taken her heart for His own possession, and rooting out all other affections, had made it as a furnace of the purest flames of love.

From heaven she now points us to the Divine Eucharist as the source of strength, of light, of love. "Consume yourself at the Eucharistic flame," she writes. "Have no soul, no heart, spirit, intention, love, life, breath, taste, but only for the Eucharist—in a word, let your entire being be ever flowing in one perpetual sacred stream towards this Jesus so unknown, so lovingly hidden in the prison of the Tabernacle. Let Him ever be our joy, our peace, our aim."

M. OLIER.

THE sixteenth century was a time when the Church of Christ mourned over the rise and increase of heresies which destroyed the faith of nations, when many religious lost their first charity and fell into apostacy, when even priests became a cause of scandal by their sin. But God in His infinite mercy interposed, and raised up a great council to give laws to monasteries, to decide matters of faith, to make rules for the reform of the clergy; and He also gave to the world in its time of need the example and influence of many saintly men and women, who should rouse the careless to greater fervour, and reawaken piety in the hearts where it had grown cold. S. Ignatius, S. Theresa, S. Charles—all had their own special and glorious work to do. But there remained still a place which was to be filled by the subject of our story—the much venerated M. Olier, wherein he should, by the institution of seminaries in France, assist in forming the character of those destined for the priesthood upon the model of Jesus Christ, and, inflaming their hearts with zeal and love, lead them on in the way of that perfection which their holy office called for.

But to do this work it was necessary for him to pass through those difficulties and those trials which should fit him to be a help to those who would need it. The labour of the missionary, the study of the theologian, the post of curé over a large and discouraging parish, formed part of his experience, as well as those spiritual joys and desolations, and the extraordinary Divine favours which God chooses for His special friends and servants.

Jean Jacques Olier was born in the city of

Paris upon the 20th of September, 1608, and was baptized the same day, receiving only the name of Jean : that of Jacques he took probably at the time of his confirmation, for he is always known by the two names.

From a very early age he showed the first sign of a vocation to the altar by his excessive love for Holy Mass and his great reverence for the ministers of God ; and at the age of seven years, being in the church of S. Antoine when the priest passed by him to the altar, such a light penetrated his mind as to the purity and sanctity required for so holy an office, that he regarded them almost as saints, who lived wholly in God, and were dead to all things earthly.

He had a very sweet and simple love for Mary Immaculate, and whenever any new clothing was prepared for him, he would run in the hat or coat, or whatever it might be, to the image of the Blessed Virgin, praying her to obtain for him the grace not to offend her Divine Son during the time he wore it.

As he grew a little older, a feeling of shame would sometimes come over him as if he had been guilty of absurdity or weakness in this practice; but if ever he missed doing it, so surely did some trouble or accident happen to himself or his new clothes, which convinced him he had been to blame in omitting his act of loving devotion.

When he was eight years old Jean Olier was sent to college, and here he delighted his masters by his industry and good conduct; but, with the liveliness and thoughtlessness of boyhood, he was the cause of a thousand alarms to his mother, and especially by walking so heedlessly along the street, that he narrowly escaped being killed upon several occasions. Madame Olier was somewhat more severe to Jean than to other children, and his lively nature seemed to her mind so unsuited to one who aspired to the priesthood, that she even thought of compelling him to abandon the idea. It happened in God's providence that S. Francis of Sales was consulted by her in her anxiety as to her son's future course, and, after describing his faults and his inclinations, she besought the holy man's advice. S. Francis promised to ask light from God respecting the boy, and one day after Mass, Madame Olier presented him and her other children to the good Bishop, that they might receive his blessing. With his usual sweetness he spoke to them one by one, and as it came to the turn of Jean, his mother explained that he was not at all a good boy, and occasioned her much sorrow and anxiety. "Do not be distressed," said S. Francis to her. "Have patience, and you will see that God is preparing this child to be a great and good servant of the Church;" and then putting his hand upon the boy's head, he embraced him, and gave him his blessing, and it seemed that God had given him all the affection of a father towards this boy during the short remainder of his holy life.

When the young Olier had reached his fourteenth year, he felt all the temptation to pleasure usual at his age, but his father watched so strictly over his actions that it was impossible for him to contract any habits of evil; and God was so good as to let a cloud come over his mind and abilities, as a punishment for any infidelity which prevented him from studying well, until he had confessed the sin. About this time Jean Olier felt a great desire to embrace a religious life, and his thoughts turned to the Carthusian Order, but he was still so young and undecided, that his true vocation seemed as yet hidden from him. Meanwhile great success attended his studies, and praise was lavished upon him for his great abilities.

At that period it was possible for men who were not priests, and had not even received holy orders, to hold the positions of priors and abbots over monasteries which their wealth could purchase; and in this way the father and mother of M. Olier, filled with a desire to see him esteemed by the world for his high standing and possessions, found means of procuring for him the title of Abbé of Pebrac, a convent in which the rule was greatly relaxed, and which needed the reform which began afterwards in so many of the religious houses in France. There his high spirits, his agreeable manners, his good connections, made him a universal favourite with worldly people, and M. Olier was drawn away so far from the Divine service which he had once set before him, that his parents repented bitterly of what their pride had done, and his mother began to pray earnestly for the conversion of her son, whom she had heedlessly thrown into temptation. The many prayers offered to God for him were the cause of the miraculous appearance of the Blessed Mère Agnes, the Dominican nun of Langrae; for it was the Divine Will that to this holy woman should be granted the joy and privilege of leading to Him the soul so gifted with power and earnestness and zeal, all of which were being choked by worldliness, but should by her prayers spring up in the strength and beauty of holiness.

These prayers soon produced a great change in the soul of him for whom they were offered, and Olier began to think very much of what life he should adopt. Probably he had already learned something of the hollowness of the world's flattery, for the old longing of his boyhood and early youth returned once more, and he prayed earnestly that God would show him whether his vocation was to a religious house or not. At this time of many doubts and constant thought, his vocation was made known to him by a special communication from God, and after due preparation he was consecrated to the Divine service in the priesthood, in the early part of the year 1633, and one of the first graces accorded to him then seems to have been that special devotion to Mary which distinguished his whole after life. He now placed himself under the guidance of S. Vincent de Paul, who desired him to give some time to prayer and recollections; and it was during this retreat that M. Olier was permitted by God to see, in vision, Agnes de Langrae, who had been praying and suffering for his soul. He was kneeling alone in his room, offering himself anew to the service of his Creator, and deploring the time he had loved too well the pleasures and honours of the world, when the Mère Agnes appeared before him, holding in one hand a crucifix and in the other a rosary. By her side was her guardian angel, and in its hand a handkerchief, on which to receive the tears which streamed from her eyes, as with a sorrowful expression she gazed upon the priest, saying, "I am weeping for thee." The gravity and sweetness of this saintly woman's appearance led M. Olier at first to suppose that the Blessed Virgin herself had deigned to visit him, for he experienced at that moment a renewed devotion to her, and seemed also to understand that in the crucifix and the rosary he should find the means of saving his soul and sanctifying his life. But the apparition was permitted him a second time, and then he comprehended that it was not Mary who came to him, but some religious of the Dominican Order who was still living, and he felt a great desire to know who she was, and in what convent she dwelt.

On coming out of his retreat, M. Olier, with some companions, undertook the fatigue and labour of a mission in the neighbourhood of Pebrac, and as he journeyed there, he heard people speaking of the virtues and holiness of the Mère Agnes, a Dominican nun, in the convent of Langrae, not far off. As her wonderful graces and gifts were mentioned, M. Olier began to wonder if this might be the religious who had appeared to him in the visions of his retreat, and he resolved to go to the convent as soon as the occupations of the mission should admit of the opportunity.

During this time God had made known to Agnes all that concerned the soul of Olier. His departure from Paris and his arrival at Pebrac, were revealed to her, and she spoke of the mission he was engaged in with so much interest and joy, that her sisters secretly wondered how she should feel these sentiments regarding one whom she did not know, and had never seen. Then they began to suspect that she had some supernatural understanding of the matter, and when M. Olier arrived as a visitor to the convent, they were more than ever certain it was so.

But though he had come to see the holy nun who had obtained for him the conversion of his life, he was disappointed, for Agnes was engaged in some duty, and did not enter the parlour; but, to the fresh surprise of her nuns, she sent her rosary as a gift to him. Several times he visited Langrae in vain; but at length Mère Agnes, accompanied by another of her sisters, came to the parlour and began speaking to him about the work he was doing in that part, as if she had no other knowledge of him than as a priest whose labours in the mission had reached her ears. But M. Olier had so strong a suspicion that Agnes de Langrae was the person who had appeared to him, that he begged her to raise her veil, which, according to the custom of her Order, concealed her face; and when she acceded to his request, he saw in a moment that he was right, and exclaimed, "Mother, I have seen you before."

"Yes, you have already seen me twice at Paris during your retreat, for I had received a command from the Blessed Virgin to pray for your conversion, as God has chosen you to lay the first foundation of a seminary in France," replied the nun.

Thus commenced that intimate spiritual friendship between these two persons, which produced, by God's blessing, such great results.

M. Olier, learning from the lips of the Mère Agnes the work God willed him to do in the Church, was anxious to learn also from her all she could tell him as to the Divine purpose in his regard; and as she had begun a work for his soul in those three years of prayer and penance, so was she permitted by her conversation and holy example to spur him on to greater love and greater self-sacrifice, and to inspire him with an attraction towards those humiliations and mortifications which are the only safe foundation of a truly spiritual life.

With what joy did this holy nun see M. Olier faithfully corresponding to each grace as it came, and advancing rapidly towards the highest path of perfection—her gratitude to Mary for having commanded her to pray for his soul broke forth in constant thanksgiving.

About this time Agnes was inspired to place herself under the guidance of M. Olier with regard to her spiritual life, and thus God gave him the means of still greater sanctification; because, as the secrets of her soul were made known to him, he became inflamed with the burning love and the deep humility which shone so brightly in her, and saw also into the wonderful ways by which God leads those who are especially chosen to receive His choicest favours.

Agnes herself regained the joy and consolation which she had felt so little during her religious life, but it was but for a short time that she was to profit by his direction, for M. Olier received an order to go to Paris, to confer as to the means of introducing a reform in the religious houses of that part. It was a trial to them both, for their friendship was great, and it had been the means of assisting each soul in the way of perfection, but neither hesitated in offering the sacrifice to God with prompt cheerfulness. At the moment of parting, the Mère Agnes gave him her crucifix, and said, "I now take leave of the parlour and of the world;" and going to prostrate herself before the Blessed Sacrament, she begged of her Lord soon to take her from earth, as the work He had given her to do was ended. It was the Will of the Almighty to answer this petition, for upon leaving the chapel Agnes was taken ill, and in a few days died a peaceful and holy death, at the age of thirty-two years.

What the Mère Agnes had begun in the soul of M. Olier was destined to be finished by the Père de Condren, General of the Oratory, who thus became his spiritual guide, although the strong tie which bound him to S. Vincent de Paul remained unbroken. It was by his direction that M. Olier went to Auvergne, to preach missions to the people, which bore great fruit. Even the little children were drawn to the love of God by his teaching, and the clergy were reawakened to increased zeal by his influence.

Just before the death of the Père de Condren, he enjoined upon M. Olier and others, whom he had been guiding, to commence their work of founding a seminary, and it was at Chartreuse that they made their first beginning; but this had to be given up and transferred to Vaurigard, where God's blessing was given to their efforts, and the little community soon increased. After a time the post of Curé of S. Sulpice was offered to M. Olier, and being directed to accept this work, he removed there, and applied himself to restore the piety and devotion of the people under his care. His great zeal was directed still to the reform of the priesthood, but he also laboured in leading the souls of many earnest men and women to a more perfect following of Christ, and persons of all ranks and conditions were helped and comforted by his instructions, so that an entire change was to be observed throughout his parish, and in all who came under his care.

To detail his own spiritual life—the mortifications, the prayers, the persecutions, the humiliations which sanctified him—would be but to repeat the history of other souls who give all to God without question, without fear; and to write the history of his work at S. Sulpice, would be impossible in so short a sketch, of years which were full of labour and of result. It only remains to glance briefly at his last years, those years of physical weakness and pain, when his great love for the Cross, his entire submission to the Divine

Will, were proved by severe trial. Although he longed for God, and heaven, and rest, he was ready to remain to suffer or to labour, and on one occasion he besought his Divine Master to restore him health, that he might use it for His glory. But he reproached himself keenly for that prayer, for no sooner had he made it than Jesus appeared to him in vision, bowed to the earth under a heavy cross, which made so great an impression upon him, that, in spite of his weakness, he rose, and prostrating himself, begged-grace to imitate his adorable Saviour, and to rejoice in sharing in the weight of His cross. As the time of his death drew near, the great mystery of the resurrection afforded him much consolation and strength, and his eyes were always fixed upon a picture of it which he had in his room. It was upon the 2nd of April that his soul passed away from earth into the presence of God, in the 49th year of his age, leaving sorrow and desolation in the hearts of all who had known and loved him. After his death this holy servant of Christ appeared in a dream to a person dwelling far from Paris, being clothed in purple, with a radiant angel by his side.

A great concourse followed his body to the tomb. His heart was separated from his body and placed in a leaden case, upon which was engraved the monograms of Jesus and Mary; his tongue was preserved in a silver box, and these two relics remain to the present day in the possession of the Seminary of S. Sulpice, as a remembrance of their father and founder.

THE END.

BY THE SAME AUTHOR.

I.

STORIES OF THE SAINTS.

Fcap 8vo. 3s. 6d.; gilt edges, 4s. 6d.

CONTENTS OF THE FIRST SERIES :—S. Frances of Rome, S. Francis of Assisi, S. Clare, S. Elizabeth of Hungary, S. Anthony of Padua, S. Benedict, S. Dominic, S. Catherine of Siena, S. Rose of Lima, S. Ignatius, S. Aloysius, S. Stanislaus Kostka, S. Agnes, S. Catherine of Alexandria, S. Cecilia, S. Laurence, S. Thomas of Canterbury, S. Philip Neri, S. Charles Borromeo, S. Vincent de Paul, S. Jane Frances de Chantal, S. Francis Xavier, S. Teresa.

II.

STORIES OF THE SAINTS.

Fcap 8vo. 3s. 6d.; gilt edges, 4s. 6d.

CONTENTS OF THE SECOND SERIES :—S. George, S. Patrick, S. Edward, K.C., S. Margaret of Scotland, S. Cuthbert, S. Dunstan, S. Gilbert of Semperingham, S. Simon Stock, S. Neot, S. Louis, King of France, S. Genevieve, S. Roch, S. Helier, S. Walburga, S. Winifride, S. Agatha, S. Lucy, S. Dorothy, S. Barbara, S. Cyr, S. Cyril, S. Zita, S. Monica, S. Lidwina, S. Germaine Cousin, S. John Nepomucene, S. John of God, S. Alexis, S. John Gualberto, S. Bernard, S. Francis of Sales.

LONDON:
R. WASHBOURNE, 18 PATERNOSTER ROW, E.C.

BY THE SAME AUTHOR.

III.
TOM'S CRUCIFIX, AND OTHER TALES.

Fcap 8vo. 3s.

CONTENTS:—Tom's Crucifix, The Old Prayer-Book, Charlie Pearson's Medal, Catherine's Promise, Norah's Temptation, Good for Evil, Joe Ryan's Repentance, Annie's First Prayer.

IV.
CATHERINE HAMILTON.

Fcap 8vo. 2s. 6d.; gilt edges, 3s.

V.
CATHERINE HAMILTON GROWN OLDER.

Fcap 8vo. 2s. 6d.; gilt edges, 3s.

VI.
IN THE PRESS.
LEGENDS FOR CATHOLIC CHILDREN.

LONDON:
R. WASHBOURNE, 18 PATERNOSTER ROW, E.C.

18 PATERNOSTER ROW, LONDON.

R. WASHBOURNE'S CATALOGUE.

JUNE 1875.

Elevations to the Heart of Jesus. By Rev. Father Doyotte, S. J. Fcap. 8vo. 3s.

Sir Thomas Maxwell and his Ward. By Miss Bridges. Fcap. 8vo. 2s.

Scraps from my Scrap Book. Fcap. 8vo. 2s. 6d.

Nano Nagle. By Rev. W. Hutch, D.D. 7s. 6d.

Thy Gods, O Israel. A Picture in Verse of the Religious Anomalies of our Time. Cr. 8vo. 2s.

Catherine grown older: a sequel to "Catherine Hamilton." By M. F. S. Fcap. 8vo. 2s. 6d.; gilt 3s.

The Eucharist and the Christian Life. By Mgr. de la Bouillerie. Translated. Fcap. 8vo. 3s. 6d.

Regina Sæculorum, or, Mary venerated in all Ages. Devotions to the Blessed Virgin from ancient sources. Fcap. 8vo. 3s.

Life of S. John of God, Founder of the Order of Hospitallers. With a Photograph, 5s.

First Communion Picture. Tastefully printed in gold and colours. Price 1s., or 10s. a dozen, *net*.

"Just what has long been wanted, a really good picture, with Tablet for First Communion and Confirmation."—*Tablet*.

Rome and her Captors. Letters collected and edited by Count Henri d'Ideville, and translated by F. R. Wegg-Prosser. Cr. 8vo. 4s.

*** *Though this Catalogue does not contain the books of other Publishers, R. W. can supply all of them, no matter by whom they are published.*

The Tradition of the Syriac Church of Antioch, concerning the Primacy and Prerogatives of S. Peter, and of his successors, the Roman Pontiffs. By the Most Rev. C. B. Benni, Syriac Archbishop of Mossul (Nineveh). 8vo. 7s. 6d.

The Supernatural Life. Translated from the French of Mgr. Mermillod, with a Preface by Lady Herbert. Cr. 8vo. 5s.

"Among the Catholic prelates on the Continent, no name stands higher than that of Dr. Mermillod, the exiled Bishop of Geneva, whose eloquence struck so forcibly the English pilgrims at Paray-le-Monial last year. . . The object of these conferences was to stir up the female portion of creation to higher and holier lives, in the hope of so influencing their husbands, their brothers, and other relatives, and so to lend a helping hand to the right side in that struggle which, as Lady Herbert so eloquently and so truly remarks, 'was formerly confined to certain places and certain minds, but is now going on all over the world—the struggle between God and the devil; between faith and unbelief; between those who still revere God's word, and the entire negation of all divine revelation.'"—*Register.*

The Jesuits, and other Essays. By Willis Nevin. Fcap. 8vo. 2s. 6d.

"If any one wishes to read in brief all that can be said about and in favour of the sons of Ignatius Loyola, by all means let him get this little work, where he will find everything ready 'at his fingers' ends.'"— *Register.* "It displays considerable vigour of thought, and no small literary power. This small book is a work of promise from one who knows both sides of those questions."—*Union Review.*

Catherine Hamilton. By the author of "Tom's Crucifix," &c. Fcap. 8vo. 2s. 6d. ; gilt, 3s.

"A short, simple, and well-told story, illustrative of the power of grace to correct bad temper in a wayward girl. For Catholic parents who are possessed with such children, we know of no better book than 'Catherine Hamilton.'"—*Register.*

Photographs (10), illustrating the history of the Miraculous Hosts, called the Blessed Sacrament of the Miracle. Price 2s. 6d. the set.

On Contemporary Prophecies. By Mgr. Dupanloup. Translated by Rev. Dr. Redmond. 8vo. 1s.

The Child. By Mgr. Dupanloup. Translated, 3s. 6d.

Protestantism and Liberty. By Professor Ozanam. Translated by W. C. Robinson. 8vo. 1s.

R. Washbourne, 18 Paternoster Row, London.

Düsseldorf Society for the Distribution of Good, Religious Pictures. R. Washbourne is now Sole Agent for Great Britain and Ireland. Yearly Subscription is 8s. 6d. *Catalogue post free.*

Düsseldorf Gallery. 8vo. half morocco, 31s. 6d. This volume contains 127 Engravings handsomely bound in half morocco, full gilt. Cash 25s.

Düsseldorf Gallery. 4to. half morocco, £5 5s. This superb work contains 331 Pictures. Handsomely bound in half morocco, full gilt.

"We confidently believe that no wealthy Catholic could possibly see the volume which we have examined and admired without ordering 'The Düsseldorf Gallery' for the adornment of his drawing-room table. . . As lovers of art, we rejoice to see what has been done, and we can only desire with all possible heartiness, that such an enterprise as this may meet with the success it deserves."—*Tablet*. "The most beautiful Catholic gift-book that was ever sent forth from the house of a Catholic publisher."—*Register*.

Catholicism, Liberalism, and Socialism. Translated from the Spanish of Donoso Cortes, by Rev. W. M'Donald. 6s.

Replies to Gladstone's "Divine Decrees."

Rome, semper eadem. By Denis Patrick Michael O'Mahony. 1s. 6d.

A Few Remarks. 6d.

Dramas, Comedies, Farces.

He would be a Lord. From the French of "Le Bourgeois Gentilhomme." Three Acts. (Boys.) 2s.

St. Louis in Chains. Drama in Five Acts, for boys. 2s.
"Well suited for acting in Catholic schools and colleges."—*Tablet*.

The Expiation. A Drama in Three Acts, for boys. 2s.
"Has its scenes laid in the days of the Crusades."—*Register*.

Shandy Maguire. A Farce for boys in Two Acts. 1s.

The Reverse of the Medal. A Drama in Four Acts, for young ladies. 6d.

Emscliff Hall: or, Two Days Spent with a Great-Aunt. A Drama in Three Acts, for young ladies. 6d.

Filiola. A Drama in Four Acts, for young ladies. 6d.

The Convent Martyr, or Callista. By Dr. Newman. Dramatized by Dr. Husenbeth. 1s.

Garden of the Soul. (WASHBOURNE'S EDITION.) *With Imprimatur of the Archbishop of Westminster.* This edition has over all others the following advantages :—1. Complete order in its arrangements. 2. Introduction of Devotions to Saint Joseph, Patron of the Church. 3. Introduction into the English Devotions for Mass to a very great extent of the Prayers from the Missal. 4. The Full Form of Administration of all the Sacraments publicly administered in Church. 5. The insertion of Indulgences above Indulgenced Prayers. 6. Its large size of type. Embossed, 1s. ; with rims, 1s. 6d. ; with Epistles and Gospels, 1s. 6d. ; with rims, 2s. French morocco, 2s. ; with rims, 2s. 6d. ; with E. and G., 2s. 6d. ; with rims, 3s. French morocco extra gilt, 2s. 6d. ; with rims, 3s. ; with E. and G., 3s. ; with rims, 3s. 6d. Calf or morocco, 4s. ; with rims, 5s. 6d. ; with E. and G., 4s. 6d.; with rims, 6s. Calf or morocco extra, 5s. ; with rims, 6s. 6d. ; with E. and G., 5s. 6d. ; with rims, 7s. Velvet, with rims, 8s., 10s. 6d., and 13s. ; with E. and G., 8s. 6d., 11s., and 13s. 6d. Russia, antique, with clasps, 12s. 6d. ; with E. and G., 13s. Ivory, 15s., 21s., 25s., and 30s. ; with E. and G., 15s. 6d., 21s. 6d., 25s. 6d., and 30s. 6d. Antique bindings, with corners and clasps: morocco, 28s., with E. and G., 28s. 6d. ; russia, 30s., with E. and G., 30s. 6d.

" This is one of the best editions we have seen of one of the best of all our Prayer-books, It is well printed in clear large type, on good paper."—*Catholic Opinion.* " A very complete arrangement of this which is emphatically-the Prayer-book of every Catholic household. It is as cheap as it is good, and we heartily recommend it."—*Universe.* " Two striking features are the admirable order displayed throughout the book and the insertion of the Indulgences, in small type above Indulgenced Prayers."—*Weekly Register.*

The Epistles and Gospels in cloth, 6d., roan, 1s. 6d.

The Little Garden. Cloth, 6d., with rims, 1s.; embossed, 9d., with rims, 1s. 3d.; roan, 1s., with rims, 1s. 6d.; french morocco, 1s. 6d., with rims, 2s.; french morocco, extra gilt, 2s., with rims, 2s. 6d.; imitation ivory, with rims, 3s.; calf or morocco, 3s., with rims, 4s.; calf or morocco, extra gilt, 4s., with rims, 5s.; velvet, with rims, 5s., 8s. 6d., 10s. 6d.; russia, with clasp, 8s.; ivory, with rims, 10s. 6d., 13s., 15s., 17s. 6d.; antique binding, with clasps : morocco, 17s. 6d., russia, 20s.; with oxydized silver or gilt mountings, in morocco case, 30s.

A Few Words from Lady Mildred's Housekeeper. 2d.
"If any of our lady readers wish to give to their servants some hint; as to the necessity of laying up some part of their wages instead of spending their money in dressing above their station, let them get 'A Few Words from Lady Mildred's Housekeeper,' and present it for the use of the servants' hall or downstairs departments. The good advice of an experienced upper servant on such subjects ought not to fall on unwilling ears."—*Register.*

Religious Reading.

"Vitis Mystica;" or, the True Vine. A Treatise on the Passion of Our Lord. Translated, with Preface, by the Rev. W. R. Bernard Brownlow. With Frontispiece. 18mo. 4s., red edges, 4s. 6d.
"It is a pity that such a beautiful treatise should for so many centuries have remained untranslated into our tongue."—*Tablet.* "It will be found very acceptable spiritual food."—*Church Herald.* "We heartily recommend it for its unction and deep sense of the beauties of nature."—*The Month.* "Full of deep spiritual lore.' —*Register.* "Every chapter of this little volume affords abundan matter for meditation."—*Universe.* "An excellent translation of beautiful treatise."—*Dublin Review.*

Ebba; or, the Supernatural Power of the Blessed Sacrament. In French. 12mo. 1s. 6d.; cloth gilt, 2s. 6d.
"The author has caught very well many of the difficulties which bar the way to the Church in this country...We may venture to hope that the work will also bear fruit on the Continent."—*The Month.* "There are thoughts in the work which we value highly."—*Dublin Review.* "It is a clever and trenchant work. . . Written in a lively and piquant style."—*Register.* "The tone of the book is kind and fervent."—*Church Herald.* "The book is exceedingly well written, and will do good to all who read it."—*Universe.*

R. Washbourne, 18 Paternoster Row, London.

Holy Places; their Sanctity and Authenticity. By the Rev. Fr. Philpin. With Maps. Crown 8vo. 6s.

"It displays an amount of patient research not often to be met with."—*Universe.* "Dean Stanley and other sinners in controversy are treated with great gentleness. They are indeed thoroughly exposed and refuted."—*Register.* "Fr. Philpin has a particularly nervous and fresh style of handling his subject, with an occasional picturesqueness of epithet or simile."—*Tablet.* "We do not question his learning and industry, and yet we cannot think them to have been uselessly expended on this work."—*Spectator.* ". . . Fr. Philpin there weighs the comparative value of extraordinary, ordinary, and natural evidence, and gives an admirable summary of the witness of the early centuries regarding the holy places of Jerusalem, with archæological and architectural proofs. It is a complete treatise of the subject."—*The Month.* "The author treats his subject with a thorough system, and a competent knowledge. It is a book of singular attractiveness and considerable merit."—*Church Herald.* "Fr. Philpin's very interesting book appears most opportunely, and at a time when pilgrimages have been revived."—*Dublin Review.*

The Consoler; or, Pious Readings addressed to the Sick and to all who are afflicted. By the Rev. P. J. Lambilotte, S.J. Translated by the Right Rev. Abbot Burder, O. Cist. Fcp. 8vo. 4s. 6d., red edges, 5s.

"As 'The Consoler' has the merit of being written in plain and simple language, and while deeply spiritual contains no higher flights into the regions of mysticism where poor and ignorant readers would be unable to follow, it is very specially adapted for one of the subjects which its writer had in view, namely, its introduction into hospitals."—*Tablet.* "A work replete with wise comfort for every affliction."—*Universe.* "A spiritual treatise of great beauty and value."—*Church Herald.*

The Souls in Purgatory. Translated from the French, by the Right Rev. Abbot Burder, O. Cist. 32mo. 3d.

"It will be found most useful as an aid to the cultivation of this especial devotion."—*Register.*

Flowers of Christian Wisdom. By Lucien Henry. With a Preface by the Right Hon. Lady Herbert of Lea. 18mo. 2s.; red edges, 2s. 6d.

"A compilation of some of the most beautiful thoughts and passages in the works of the Fathers, the great schoolmen, and eminent modern Churchmen, and will probably secure a good circulation."—*Church Times.* "It is a compilation of gems of thought, carefully selected."—*Tablet.* "It is a small but exquisite bouquet, like that which S. Francis of Sales has prepared for *Philothea.*"—*Universe.*

Apostleship of Prayer. By Rev. H. Ramière. 6s.
The Happiness of Heaven. By a Father of the Society of Jesus. Fcap. 8vo. 4s.
God our Father. By the same Author. Fcap. 8vo. 4s.
The Light of the Holy Spirit in the World. By the Rev. Canon Hedley, O.S.B. 1s.; cloth, 1s. 6d.
A General History of the Catholic Church: from the commencement of the Christian Era until the present time. By the Abbé Darras. 4 vols., large 8vo. cloth, 48s.
The Book of Perpetual Adoration; or, the Love of Jesus in the most Holy Sacrament of the Altar. By Mgr. Boudon. Edited by the Rev. J. Redman, D.D. Fcap. 8vo. 3s.; red edges, 3s. 6d.

"This new translation is one of Boudon's most beautiful works, ... and merits that welcome in no ordinary degree."—*Tablet.* "The devotions at the end will be very acceptable aids in visiting the Blessed Sacrament, and there are two excellent methods for assisting at Mass."—*The Month.* "It has been pronounced by a learned and pious French priest to be 'the most beautiful of all books written in honour of the Blessed Sacrament."—*The Nation.*

Spiritual Works of Louis of Blois, Abbot of Liesse. Edited by the Rev. John Edward Bowden, of the Oratory. Fcap. 8vo. 3s. 6d; red edges, 4s.

"No more important or welcome addition could have been made to our English ascetical literature than this little book. It is a model of good translation."—*Dublin Review.* "This handy little volume will certainly become a favourite."—*Tablet.* "Elegant and flowing."—*Register.* "Most useful of meditations."—*Catholic Opinion.*

Heaven Opened by the Practice of Frequent Confession and Communion. By the Abbé Favre. Translated from the French, carefully revised by a Father of the Society of Jesus. Third Edition. Fcap. 8vo. 3s. 6d.; red edges, 4s. Cheap edit. 2s.

"This beautiful little book of devotion. We may recommend it to the clergy as well as to the laity."—*Tablet.* "It is filled with quotations from the Holy Scriptures, the Fathers, and the Councils of the Church, and thus will be found of material assistance to the clergy, as a storehouse of doctrinal and ascetical authorities on the two great sacraments of Holy Eucharist and Penance."—*Register.*

R. Washbourne, 18 Paternoster Row, London.

The Spiritual Life. — Conferences delivered to the *Enfants de Marie* by Père Ravignan. Cr. 8vo. 5s.

"Père Ravignan's words are as applicable to the ladies of London as to those of Paris. They could not have a better book for their spiritual reading."—*Tablet.* "A depth of eloquence and power of exhortation which few living preachers can rival."—*Church Review.*

Lenten Thoughts. Drawn from the Gospel for each day in Lent. By the Bishop of Northampton. 1s. 6d.; stronger bound, 2s.; red edges, 2s. 6d.

"A beautiful little volume of Meditations."—*Universe.* "Will be found a useful manual."—*Tablet.* "An admirable little book.' —*Nation.* "Clear and practical."—*The Month.* "A very beautiful and sipmle little book."—*Church Herald.*

Holy Communion: it is my Life. By H. Lebon. 4s.

Contemplations on the Most Holy Sacrament of the Altar, drawn from the Sacred Scriptures. 18mo. cloth, 2s.; cloth extra, red edges, 2s. 6d.

"This is a welcome addition to our books of Scriptural devotion. It contains thirty-four excellent subjects of reflection before the Blessed Sacrament, or for making a spiritual visit to the Blessed Sacrament at home; for the use of the sick."—*Dublin Review.*

Good Thoughts for Priests and People; or Short Meditations for Every Day in the Year. By Rev. T. Noethen. 12mo. 8s.

One Hundred Pious Reflections. Extracted from Alban Butler's "Lives of the Saints." 18mo. cloth, red edges, 2s.; cheap edition, 1s.

"A happy idea. The author of 'The Lives of the Saints' had a way of breathing into his language the unction and force which carries the truth of the Gospel into the heart."—*Letter to the Editor from* THE RIGHT REV. DR. ULLATHORNE, BISHOP OF BIRMINGHAM. "Well selected, sufficiently short, and printed in good bold type."—*Tablet.* "Good, sound, practical."—*Church Herald.*

The Imitation of Christ. With reflections. 32mo. 1s. Persian calf, 3s. 6d. Also an Edition with ornamental borders. Fcap. cloth, red edges, 3s. 6d.

Following of Christ. Small pocket edition, 1s. cloth; 1s. 6d. embossed; roan, 2s; French morocco, 2s. 6d.; calf or morocco, 4s. 6d.; calf or morocco extra gilt, 5s. 6d.; ivory, 15s. and 16s.; morocco, antique, 17s. 6d.; russia antique, 20s.

Conversion of the Teutonic Race. By Mrs. Hope, author of "Early Martyrs." Edited by the Rev. Father Dalgairns. 2 vols. crown 8vo. 12s.
I. Conversion of the Franks and the English, 6s.
II. S. Boniface and the Conversion of Germany, 6s.

"It is good in itself, possessing considerable literary merit; it forms one of the few Catholic books brought out in this country which are not translations or adaptations."—*Dublin Review.* "It is a great thing to find a writer of a book of this class so clearly grasping, and so boldly setting forth truths, which, familiar as they are to scholars, are still utterly unknown by most of the writers of our smaller literature."—*Saturday Review.* "A very valuable work .... Mrs. Hope has compiled an original history, which gives constant evidence of great erudition, and sound historical judgment."—*Month.* "This is a most taking book: it is solid history and romance in one."—*Catholic Opinion.* "It is carefully, and in many parts beautifully written."—*Universe.*

Cistercian Order: its Mission and Spirit. Comprising the Life of S. Robert of Newminster, and the Life of S. Robert of Knaresborough. By the author of "Cistercian Legends." Crown 8vo. 3s. 6d.

Cistercian Legends of the 13th Century. Translated from the Latin by the Rev. Henry Collins. 3s.

"Interesting records of Cistercian sanctity and cloistral experience."—*Dublin Review.* "A casquet of jewels."—*Weekly Register.* "Most beautiful legends, full of deep spiritual reading."—*Tablet.* "Well translated, and beautifully got up."—*Month.* "A compilation of anecdotes, full of heavenly wisdom."—*Catholic Opinion.*

The Directorium Asceticum; or Guide to the Spiritual Life. By Scaramelli. Translated and edited at St. Beuno's College. 4 vols. crown 8vo. 24s.

Maxims of the Kingdom of Heaven. New and enlarged Edition. 5s.; red edges, 5s. 6d.; calf or morocco, 10s. 6d.

"The selections on every subject are numerous, and the order and arrangement of the chapters will greatly facilitate meditation and reference."—*Freeman's Journal.* "We are glad to see that this admirable devotional work, of which we have before spoken in warm paise, has reached a second issue."—*Weekly Register.* "It has an Introduction by J. H. N., and bears the Imprimatur of the Archbishop of Westminster. We need say no more in its praise."—*Tablet.* "A most beautiful little book."—*Catholic Opinion.* "This priceless volume."—*Universe.* "Most suitable for meditation and reference."—*Dublin Review.*

R. Washbourne, 18 Paternoster Row, London.

The Oxford Undergraduate of Twenty Years Ago: his Religion, his Studies, his Antics. By a Bachelor of Arts. [Author of "The Comedy of Convocation."] 2s. 6d. ; cloth, 3s. 6d.

"The writing is full of brilliancy and point."—*Tablet.* "Time has not dimmed the author's recollection, and has no doubt served to sharpen his sense of undergraduate humour and his reading of undergraduate character."—*Examiner.* "It will deservedly attract attention, not only by the briskness and liveliness of its style, but also by the accuracy of the picture which it probably gives of an individual experience."—*The Month.* "Whoever takes this book in hand will read it through and through with the keenest pleasure and with great benefit."—*Universe.*

The Infallibility of the Pope. A Lecture. By the same Author. 8vo. 1s.

"A splendid lecture, by one who thoroughly understands his subject, and in addition is possessed of a rare power of language in which to put before others what he himself knows so well."—*Universe.* "There are few writers so well able to make things plain and intelligible as the author of 'The Comedy of Convocation.'... The lecture is a model of argument and style."—*Register.*

Comedy of Convocation in the English Church. Edited by Archdeacon Chasuble, D.D. 2s. 6d.

Reply to the Bishop of Ripon's Attack on the Catholic Church. By the same Author. 6d.

The Harmony of Anglicanism. Report of a Conference on Church Defence. [By T. W. M. Marshall, Esq.] 8vo. 2s. 6d.

"'Church Defence' is characterized by the same caustic irony, the same good-natured satire, the same logical acuteness which distinguished its predecessor, the 'Comedy of Convocation.'... A more scathing bit of irony we have seldom met with."—*Tablet.* "Clever, humorous, witty, learned, written by a keen but sarcastic observer of the Establishment, it is calculated to make defenders wince as much as it is to make all others smile."—*Nonconformist.*

The Roman Question. By Dr. Husenbeth. 1s.

Consoling Thoughts of St. Francis de Sales. By Père Huguet. 18mo., 2s.

Holy Readings. Short Selections from well-known Authors. By J. R. Digby Beste, Esq. 32mo. cloth, 2s. ; cloth, red edges, 2s. 6d. ; roan, 3s. morocco, 6s. [See "Catholic Hours," p. 23.]

St. Peter; his Name and his Office as set forth in
Holy Scripture. By T. W. Allies. *Second Edition.* Revised. Crown 8vo. 5s.
"A standard work. There is no single book in English, on the Catholic side, which contains the Scriptural argument about St. Peter and the Papacy so clearly or conclusively put."—*Month.*
"An admirable volume."—*The Universe.* "This valuable work." —*Weekly Register.* "A second edition, with a new and very touching preface."—*Dublin Review.*

The Life of Pleasure. Translated from the French of Mgr. Dechamps. Fcap. 8vo. 1s. 6d.

Sure Way to Heaven: a little Manual for Confession and Holy Communion. 32mo. cloth, 6d. Persian 2s. 6d. Calf or morocco, 3s. 6d.

Compendium of the History of the Catholic Church. By Rev. T. Noethen. 12mo. 8s.

History of the Catholic Church, for schools. By Rev. T. Noethen. 12mo. 5s. 6d.

Anti-Janus. Translated from the German of Dr. Hergenröther, by Professor Robertson. 4s.

Benedictine Almanack. Yearly. Price 1d.

Catholic Calendar and Guide to the Services of the Church. Yearly. Price 4d. and 6d.

Catholic Directory for Scotland. Yearly. 1s.

Dr. Pusey's Eirenicon considered in Relation to Catholic Unity. By H. N. Oxenham. 2s. 6d.

Sancti Alphonsi Doctoris Officium Parvum—Novena and Little Office in honour of St. Alphonsus. Fcap. 8vo. 1s.; cloth, 2s.; cloth extra, 3s.

Familiar Instructions on Christian Truths. By a Priest. No. 1, Detraction. 4d. No. 2, The Dignity of the Priesthood. 3d. No. 3, Necessity of hearing the Word of God. Why it produces no fruit, and how to be heard. On the necessity of Faith. 3d.

Sweetness of Holy Living; or Honey culled from the Flower Garden of S. Francis of Sales. 1s. French morocco, 3s.
"In it will be found some excellent aids to devotion and meditation."—*Weekly Register.*

Commonitory of S. Vincent of Lerins. 12mo. 1s. 3d.

Men and Women of the English Reformation, from the days of Wolsey to the death of Cranmer. By S. H. Burke, M.A. 2 vols. 13s. Vol. ii., 6s. 6d.

"It contains a great amount of curious and useful information, gathered together with evident care."—*Dublin Review.* "Interesting and valuable."—*Tablet.* "It is, in truth, the only dispassionate record of a much contested epoch we have ever read."—*Cosmopolitan.* "It is so forcibly, but truthfully written, that it should be in the hands of every seeker after truth."—*Catholic Opinion.*—"On all hands admitted to be one of the most valuable historical works ever published."—*Nation.* "The author produces evidence that cannot be gainsayed."—*Universe.* "Full of interest, and very temperately written."—*Church Review.* "Able, fairly impartial, and likely to be of considerable value to the student of history. Replete with information."—*Church Times.* "The book supplies many hitherto unknown facts of the times of which it is a history."—*Church Opinion.* "A clever and well-written historical statement of facts concerning the chief actors of our so-called Reformation."—*The Month.*

Père Lacordaire's Conferences. God, 6s. Jesus Christ, 6s. God and Man, 6s.

A Devout Paraphrase on the Seven Penitential Psalms; or, a Practical Guide to Repentance. By the Rev. Fr. Blyth. To which is added:—Necessity of Purifying the Soul, by St. Francis of Sales. 18mo., 1s. 6d.; red edges, 2s.; cheap edition, 1s.

"A new edition of a book well known to our grandfathers. The work is full of devotion and of the spirit of prayer."—*Universe.* "A very excellent work, and ought to be in the hands of every Catholic."—*Waterford News.*

A New Miracle at Rome; through the Intercession of Blessed John Berchmans. 2d.

Cure of Blindness; through the Intercession of Our Lady and St. Ignatius. 2d.

BY THE POOR CLARES OF KENMARE.

Woman's Work in Modern Society. 7s. 6d.
A Nun's Advice to her Girls. 2s. 6d.
Daily Steps to Heaven. Fcap. 8vo. 4s. 6d.
Book of the Blessed Ones. 4s. 6d.
Jesus and Jerusalem; or, the Way Home. 4s. 6d.
The Spouse of Christ. Crown 8vo. 7s. 6d.
The Ecclesiastical Year. Fcap. 4s. 6d.; calf, 6s. 6d.

Sermons, Lectures, &c. By Rev. M. B. Buckley. 6s.
A Homely Discourse ; Mary Magdalen. Cr. 8vo. 6d.
Extemporaneous Speaking. By Rev. T. J. Potter. 5s.
Pastor and People. By Rev. T. J. Potter. 6s.
Eight Short Sermon Essays. By Dr. Redmond. 1s.
One Hundred Short Sermons. By Rev. H. T. Thomas. 8vo. 12s.
Catholic Sermons. By Father Burke, and others. 2s.
Non Possumus ; or, the Temporal Sovereignty of the Popes. By the Rev. Father Lockhart. 1s.
Secession or Schism. By Fr. Lockhart. 6d.
Who is the Anti-Christ of Prophecy? By the Rev. Fr. Lockhart. 1s.
The Communion of Saints. By the Rev. Father Lockhart. 1s. ; cloth, 1s. 6d.
The Church of England and its Defenders. By the Rev. W. R. Bernard Brownlow. 8vo. 1st Letter, 6d. ; 2nd Letter, 1s.
Lyrics of Light and Life. XLIII original poems, by Dr. Newman and others. 5s.
Lectures on the Life, Writings, and Times of Edmund Burke. By Professor Robertson. 5s.
Professor Robertson's Lectures on Modern History and Biography. Crown 8vo. cloth, 6s.
The Knight of the Faith. By the Rev. Dr. Laing.
1. A Favourite Fallacy about Private Judgment. 1d.
2. Catholic not Roman Catholic. 4d.
3. Rationale of the Mass. 1s.
4. Challenge to the Churches of England, Scotland, and all Protestant Denominations. 1d.
5. Absurd Protestant Opinions concerning *Intention*, and Spelling Book of Christian Philosophy. 4d.
6. Whence the Monarch's right to rule. 2s. 6d.
7. Protestantism against the Natural Moral Law. 1d.
8. What is Christianity? 6d.
Abridged Explanation of the Medal or Cross of S. Benedict. 1d.

Diary of a Confessor of the Faith. 12mo. 1s.
Sursum, 1s. Homeward, 2s. Both by Rev. Fr. Rawes.
Sermon at the Month's Mind of the Most Rev. Dr. Spalding, Archbishop of Baltimore. 1s.
Commentary on the Psalms. By Bellarmin. 4to. 4s.
Monastic Legends. By E. G. K. Browne. 8vo. 6d.

BY DR. MANNING, ARCHBISHOP OF WESTMINSTER.

The Convocation in Crown and Council. 6d. net.
Confidence in God. Fcap. 1s.; cloth, 1s. 6d.
Temporal Sovereignty of the Popes. 1s.; cloth, 1s. 6d.
The Church, the Spirit, and the Word. 6d.

BY THE PASSIONIST FATHERS.

The School of Jesus Crucified. 3s. 6d.; morocco, 5s.
The Manual of the Cross and Passion. 32mo. 2s. 6d.
The Manual of the Seven Dolours. 32mo. 1s. 6d.
The Christian Armed. 32mo. 1s. 6d.; mor. 3s. 6d.
Guide to Sacred Eloquence. 2s.

Religious Instruction.

The Catechism, Illustrated with Passages from the Holy Scriptures. Arranged by the Rev. J. B. Bagshawe, with Imprimatur. Crown 8vo. 2s. 6d.

"I believe the Catechism to be one of the best possible books of controversy, to those, at least, who are inquiring with a real desire to find the truth."—*Extract from the Preface.*

"An excellent idea. The very thing of all others that is needed by many under instruction."—*Tablet.* "It is a book which will do incalculable good. Our priests will hail with pleasure so valuable a help to their weekly instructions in the Catechism, while in schools its value will be equally recognized."—*Weekly Register.* "A work of great merit."—*Church Herald.* "We can hardly wish for anything better, either in intention or in performance."—*The Month.* "Very valuable."—*Dublin Review.*

A Dogmatic Catechism. By Frassinetti. Translated from the original Italian by the Oblate Fathers of St. Charles. With a Preface by His Grace the Archbishop of Westminster. Fcap. 8vo. 3s.

"We give a few extracts from Frassinetti's work, as samples of its excellent execution."—*Dublin Review.* "Needs no commendation."—*Month.* "It will be found useful, not only to catechists, but also for the instruction of converts from the middle class of society."—*Tablet.*

The Threshold of the Catholic Church. A course of Plain Instructions for those entering her Communion. By Rev. J. B. Bagshawe. Cr. 8vo. 4s.

"A scholarly, well-written book, full of information."—*Church Herald.* "An admirable book, which will be of infinite service to thousands."—*Universe.* "Plain, practical, and unpretentious, it exhausts so entirely the various subjects of instruction necessary for our converts, that few missionary priests will care to dispense with its assistance."—*Register.* "It has very special merits of its own. . It is the work, not only of a thoughtful writer and good theologian, but of a wise and experienced priest."—*Dublin Review.* "Its characteristic is the singular simplicity and clearness with which everything is explained. . . It will save priests hours and days of time."—*Tablet.* "There is much in it with which we thoroughly agree."—*Church Times.* "There was a great want of a manual of instruction for convents, and the want has now been supplied, and in the most satisfactory manner."—*The Month.*

The Catechism of Christian Doctrine. Approved for the use of the Faithful in all the Dioceses of England and Wales. Price 1d. ; cloth, 2d.

A First Sequel to the Catechism. By the Rev. J. Nary. 32mo. 1d.

"It will recommend itself to teachers in Catholic schools as one peculiarly adapted to the use of such children as have mastered the Catechism, and yet have nothing else to fall back upon for higher religious instruction. It will be found a great assistance as well to teachers as to pupils who belong to the higher standards in our Catholic poor schools."—*Weekly Register.*

Catechism made Easy. A Familiar Explanation of "The Catechism of Christian Doctrine." By Rev. H. Gibson. Vol. I., 4s. Vol. II., 4s.

The Seven Sacraments explained and defended. Edited by a Catholic Clergyman. 1s. 6d.

Burton's Ecclesiastical History. 1s.

Protestant Principles Examined by the Written Word. Originally entitled, "The Protestant's Trial by the Written Word." *New edition.* 18mo. 1s.

"An excellent book."—*Church News.* "A good specimen of the concise controversial writing of English Catholics in the early part of the seventeenth century."—*Catholic Opinion.* "A little book which might be consulted profitably by any Catholic."—*Church Times.* "A clever little manual."—*Westminster Gazette.* "A useful little volume."—*The Month.* "An excellent little book."—*Weekly Register.* "A well-written and well-argued treatise."—*Tablet.*

R. Washbourne, 18 Paternoster Row, London.

Descriptive Guide to the Mass. By the Rev. Dr. Laing. 1s.; extra cloth, 1s. 6d.

"An attempt to exhibit the structure of the Mass. The logical relation of parts is ingeniously effected by an elaborate employment of differences of type, so that the classification, down to the minutest subdivision, may at once be caught by the eye."—*Tablet.*

The Necessity of Enquiry as to Religion. By Henry John Pye, M.A. 4d.; for distribution, 20s. a hundred; cloth, 6d.

"Mr. Pye is particularly plain and straightforward."—*Tablet.* "It is calculated to do much good. We recommend it to the clergy, and think it a most useful work to place in the hands of all who are under instruction."—*Westminster Gazette.* "A thoroughly searching little pamphlet."—*Universe.* "A clever little pamphlet. Each point is treated briefly and clearly."—*Catholic Opinion.*

A General Catechism of the Christian Doctrine. By the Right Rev. Dr. Poirier. 18mo. 9d.

The Grounds of Catholic Doctrine. By Dr. Challoner. Large type edition. 18mo. cloth, 4d.

Dr. Butler's *First* Catechism, ½d. *Second* Catechism, 1d.; *Third* Catechism, 1½d.

Dr. Doyle's Catechism, 1½d.

Lessons on the Christian Doctrine, 1d.

Fleury's Historical Catechism. Large edition, 1½d.

Bible History for the use of Catholic Schools and Families. By the Rev. R. Gilmour. 2s.

Herder's Prints—Old and New Testament. 40 large coloured pictures. 12s.

Origin and Progress of Religious Orders, and Happiness of a Religious State. By Fr. Jerome Platus, S.J.; translated by Patrick Mannock. Fcap. 8vo. 2s. 6d.

"The whole work is evidently calculated to impress any reader with the great advantages attached to a religious life."—*Register.*

Children of Mary in the World. 32mo. 1d.

The Christian Teacher. By Ven. de la Salle. 1s. 8d.

Christian Politeness. By the Ven. de la Salle. 1s.

Duties of a Christian. By the Ven. de la Salle. 2s.

The Monks of Iona and the Duke of Argyll. By the Rev. J. Stewart M'Corry, D.D. 8vo. 3s. 6d.

R. Washbourne, 18 Paternoster Row, London.

The Young Catholic's Guide to Confession and Holy Communion. By Dr. Kenny. *Third edition.* Paper, 4d. ; cloth, 6d. ; cloth, red edges, 9d.

"Admirably suited to the purpose for which it is intended."—*Weekly Register.* "One of the best we have seen. The instructions are clear, pointed, and devout, and the prayers simple, well constructed, and sufficiently brief. We recommend it."—*Church News.*

Practical Counsels for Holy Communion. By Mgr. de Ségur. Translated for children, 9d.

Pactical Counsels on Confession. By Mgr. de Ségur. Translated for children. 6d.

Instructions for the Sacrament of Confirmation. 6d.

Auricular Confession. By Rev. Dr. Melia. 1s. 6d.

Explanation of the Epistles and Gospels, &c. By the Rev. Fr. Goffine. Illustrated. 7s.

Rules for a Christian Life. By S. Charles Borromeo. 2d.

Anglican Orders. By the Very Rev. Canon Williams. *Second Edition.* Crown 8vo. 3s. 6d.

The Rainy Day, and Guild of Our Lady. By the Rev. Fr. Richardson. 2d.

Little by Little ; or, the Penny Bank. By the Rev. Fr. Richardson. 1d.

The Crusade, or Catholic Association for the Suppression of Drunkenness. By the same. 1d.

Lives of Saints, &c.

Life of the Ven. Anna Maria Taigi. Translated from the French of Calixte, by A. V. Smith Sligo. 8vo. 5s.

"A most valuable book."—*Dublin Review.* "An edifying and delightful book of spiritual reading."—*Church Herald.* "We hope to see it meet with that success which works of the sort have a right to expect."—*Westminster Gazette.* "The translator's labour has been so ably performed that the book is wanting in few of the merits of an original work."—*Tablet.*

Butler's Lives of the Saints. 2 vols., 8vo., cloth, 28s. ; or in cloth gilt, 34s. ; or in 4 vols., 8vo., cloth, 32s. ; or in cloth gilt, 48s. ; or in leather gilt, 64s.

Life, Passion, Death, and Resurrection of Our Blessed Lord. Translated from Ribadeneira. 1s.

Oratorian Lives of the Saints. Second Series. Post 8vo.
    Vol. I. S. Bernardine of Siena. 5s.
    Vol. II.—S. Philip Benizi. 5s.
    Vol. III.—S. Veronica Giuliani, and Blessed Battista Varani. 5s.
    Vol. IV.—S. John of God. 5s.

⁴ The works translated from will be in most cases the Lives drawn up *for* or *from* the processes of canonization or beatification, as being more full, more authentic, and more replete with anecdote, thus enabling the reader to become better acquainted with the Saint's disposition and spirit; while the simple matter-of-fact style of the narrative is, from its unobtrusive character, more adapted for spiritual reading than the views and generalizations, and prologetic extenuations of more recent biographers. The work is published with the permission and approval of superiors. Every volume containing the Life of a person not yet canonized or beatified by the Church will be prefaced by a protest in conformity with the decree of Urban VIII., and in all Lives which introduce questions of mystical theology great care will be taken to publish nothing which has not had adequate sanction, or without the reader being informed of the nature and amount of the sanction. Each volume is embellished with a Portrait of the Saint.

Life of Sister Mary Cherubina Clare of S. Francis, Translated from the Italian, with Preface by Lady Herbert. Cr. 8vo. with Photograph, 3s. 6d.

Stories of the Saints. By M. F. S., author of "Tom's Crucifix, and other Tales," "Catherine Hamilton," &c. Fcap. 8vo. 2 vols., each 3s. 6d., gilt, 4s. 6d.

Life of B. Giovanni Colombini. By Feo Belcari. Translated from the editions of 1541 and 1832. with a Photograph. Cr. 8vo. 3s. 6d.

Sketch of the Life and Letters of the Countess Adelstan. By E. A. M., author of "Rosalie, or the Memoirs of a French Child," "Life of Paul Seigneret, &c." 2s. 6d.

DR. NEWMAN'S LIVES OF THE ENGLISH SAINTS.
Life of St. Augustine of Canterbury. 12mo. 3s. 6d.
Life of St. German. 12mo. cloth, 3s. 6d.
Life of Stephen Langton. 12mo. cloth, 2s. 6d.

Life of St. Boniface, and the Conversion of Germany. By Mrs. Hope. Edited, with a Preface, by the Rev. Father Dalgairns. Cr. 8vo. 6s.

"Every one knows the story of S. Boniface's martyrdom, but every one has not heard it so stirringly set forth as in her 22nd chapter by Mrs. Hope."—*Dublin Review.*

Louise Lateau: her Life, Stigmata, and Ecstasies. By Dr. Lefebvre. Translated from the French by T. S. Shepard. Fcap. 8vo. 2s.

Venerable Mary Christina of Savoy. 6d.

Memoirs of a Guardian Angel. Fcap. 8vo. 4s.

Life of St. Patrick. 12mo. 1s.

Life of St. Bridget, and of other Saints of Ireland. 1s.

Insula Sanctorum: the Island of Saints. 1s.; cloth, 2s.

Life of Paul Seigneret, Seminarist of Saint-Sulpice. Fcap. 8vo., 1s.; cloth extra, 1s. 6d.; gilt, 2s.

"An affecting and well-told narrative... It will be a great favourite, especially with our pure-minded, high-spirited young people."—*Universe.* "Paul Seigneret was remarkable for the simplicity and the heroism of both his natural and his religious character."—*Tablet.* "We commend it to parents with sons under their care, and especially do we recommend it to those who are charged with the education and training of our Catholic youth."—*Register.*

A Daughter of St. Dominic. By Grace Ramsay. Fcap. 8vo. 1s. 6d.; cloth extra, 2s.

"A beautiful little work. The narrative is highly interesting."—*Dublin Review.* "It is full of courage and faith and Catholic heroism."—*Universe.* "One who has lived and died in our own day, who led the common life of every one else, but yet who learned how to supernaturalize this life in so extraordinary a way that we forget 'the doctor's daughter in a provincial town,' while reading Grace Ramsay's beautiful picture of the wonders effected by her ubiquitous charity, and still more by her fervent prayer."—*Tablet.* "The spirit of thorough devotion to Rome manifest in every page of this charming work will render it most attractive to Leaguers of St. Sebastian."—*The Crusader.*

The Glory of St. Vincent de Paul. By the Most Rev. Dr. Manning, Archbishop of Westminster. 1s.

Life of S. Edmund of Canterbury. From the French of the Rev. Father Massé, S. J. By George White. Cloth, 1s. ad

Life of Dr. Grant, first Bishop of Southwark. By Grace Ramsay. 8vo. 16s.

The Life of St. Francis of Assisi. Translated from the Italian of St. Bonaventure by Miss Lockhart. With a Preface by His Grace the Archbishop of Westminster. Fcap. 8vo. cloth, 2s. and 3s.; gilt, 4s.
"It is beautifully translated."—*Catholic Opinion.* "A most interesting and instructive volume."—*Tablet.* "This is a first-rate translation by one of the very few persons who have the art of translating as if they were writing an original work."—*Dublin Review.*

Life of Fr. de Ravignan. Crown 8vo. 9s.
The Pilgrimage to Paray le Monial, with a brief notice of the Blessed Margaret Mary. 6d.
Patron Saints. By Eliza Allen Starr. Cr. 8vo. 10s.
His Eminence Cardinal Wiseman; with full account of his Obsequies; Funeral Oration by Archbishop Manning, &c. 1s.; cloth, red edges, 1s. 6d.
Count de Montalembert. By George White. 6d.
Life of Mgr. Weedall. By Dr. Husenbeth. 3s. 6d.
Life of Pope Pius IX. 6d. Cheap edition, 1d.
Challoner's Memoirs of Missionary Priests. 8vo. 6s.

BY THE POOR CLARES OF KENMARE.

Life of Father Matthew. 2s. 6d.
Life and Revelations of St. Gertrude. Cr. 8vo. 7s. 6d.
Spirit of St. Gertrude. 18mo. 2s. 6d.
Life of St. Aloysius. 6d.; St. Joseph, 6d., cloth, 9d.; St. Patrick, 6d., cloth, 9d.
Life of St. Patrick. Illustrated by Doyle. 4to. 20s.

Our Lady.

Readings for the Feasts of Our Lady, and especially for the Month of May. By the Rev. A. P. Bethell. 18mo. 1s. 6d.; cheap edition, 1s.
The History of the Blessed Virgin. By the Abbé Orsini. Translated from the French by the Very Rev. F. C. Husenbeth, D.D. With eight Illustrations. Crown 8vo. 3s. 6d.
Manual of Devotions in Honour of Our Lady of Sorrows. Compiled by the Clergy at St. Patrick's Soho. 18mo. 1s.; cloth, red edges, 1s. 6d.
Life of Our Lady in Verse. 2s.

Devotion to Our Lady in North America. By the Rev. Xavier Donald Macleod. 8vo. 5s. *cash*.

"The work of an author than whom few more gifted writers have ever appeared among us. It is not merely a religious work, but it has all the charms of an entertaining book of travels. We can hardly find words to express our high admiration of it."—*Weekly Register*.

Life of the Ever-Blessed Virgin. Proposed as a Model to Christian Women. 1s.

Our Blessed Lady of Lourdes: a Faithful Narrative of the Apparitions of the Blessed Virgin Mary at the Rocks of Massabielle, near Lourdes, in the year 1858. By F. C. Husenbeth, D.D., V.G., and Provost of Northampton. 18mo. 6d.; cloth, 1s.; with Novena, 1s.; cloth, 1s. 6d. Novena, separately, 4d.; Litany, 1d., or 6s. per 100.

The Blessed Virgin's Root traced in the Tribe of Ephraim. By the Rev. Dr. Laing. 8vo. 10s. 6d.

Month of Mary for Interior Souls. By M. A. Macdaniel. 18mo. 2s.

Month of Mary, principally for the use of religious communities. 18mo. 1s. 6d.

A Devout Exercise in Honour of the Blessed Virgin Mary. From the Psalter and Prayers of S. Bonaventure. In Latin and English, with Indulgences applicable to the Holy Souls. 32mo. 1s.

The Definition of the Immaculate Conception. 6d.

The Little Office of the Immaculate Conception. In Latin and English. By the Very Rev. Dr. Husenbeth. 32mo. 4d.; cloth, 6d.; roan, 1s.; calf or morocco, 2s. 6d.

Our Lady's Lament, and the Lamentation of St. Mary Magdalene. 2s.

The Virgin Mary. By Dr. Melia. 8vo. 11s. 3d. *cash*.

Archconfraternity of Our Lady of Angels. 1s. per 100.

Litany of Our Lady of Angels. 1s. per 100.

Concise Portrait of the Blessed Virgin. 1s. per 100.

Origin of the Blue Scapular. 1d.

Miraculous Prayer—August Queen of Angels. 1s. 100.

Prayer-Books.

Washbourne's Edition of the "Garden of the Soul," in medium-sized type (small type as a rule being avoided). For prices see page 4.

The Little Garden. 6d., and upwards. *See page* 5.

The Lily of St. Joseph; a little Manual of Prayers and Hymns for Mass. Price 2d.; cloth, 3d.; or with gilt lettering, 4d.; more strongly bound, 6d.; or with gilt edges, 8d.; roan, 1s.; French morocco, 1s. 6d.; calf, or morocco, 2s.; gilt, 2s. 6d.

"It supplies a want which has long been felt; a prayer-book for children, which is not a childish book, a handy book for boys and girls, and for men and women too, if they wish for a short, easy-to-read, and devotional prayer-book."—*Catholic Opinion*. "A very complete prayer-book. It will be found very useful for children and for travellers."—*Weekly Register*. "A neat little compilation, which will be specially useful to our Catholic School-children. The hymns it contains are some of Fr. Faber's best."—*Universe*.

Life of Our Lord Commemorated in the Mass; a Method of Assisting at the Holy Sacrifice. By the Rev. E. G. Bagshawe, of the Oratory. 32mo. 3d.; cloth, 4d.; roan, 1s.; French morocco, 1s. 6d.; calf or morocco, 2s. 6d.

Path to Paradise. 36 full page Illustrations. Cloth, 3d. With 50 Illustrations, cloth, 4d.

Manual of Catholic Devotion. 6d.; roan, 1s. 6d.; calf or morocco, 2s. 6d.

Ursuline Manual. Persian calf, 7s. 6d.; morocco, 10s.

Crown of Jesus. Persian calf, 6s.; morocco, 7s. 6d. and 8s. 6d., with rims, 10s. 6d.; morocco, extra gilt, 10s. 6d., with rims, 12s. 6d.; ivory, with rims, 21s., 25s., 27s. 6d. and 30s.

Burial of the Dead (Adults and Infants) in Latin and English. Royal 32mo. cloth, 6d.; roan, 1s. 6d.

"Being in a portable form, will be found useful by those who are called upon to assist at that solemn rite."—*Tablet*.

In Suffragiis Sanctorum. Commem S. Josephi. Commem S. Georgii. Set of five for 4d.

Paradise of God; or Virtues of the Sacred Heart. 4s.
Devotions to the Sacred Heart. By the Rev. S. Franco. 4s., paper covers, 2s.
Devotions to the Sacred Heart. By the Rev. J. Joy Dean. Fcap. 8vo. 3s.
Devotions to Sacred Heart of Jesus. By the Rt. Rev. Dr. Milner. *New Edition*. To which is added Devotions to the Immaculate Heart of Mary. 3d.; cloth, 6d.; gilt, 1s.
Pleadings of the Sacred Heart. 18mo. 1s.
Sacred Heart of Jesus offered to the Piety of the Young engaged in Study. By Rev. A. Deham, S.J. 6d.
"Complete little Manual of Devotion to the Sacred Heart, and as such will be valued by Catholics of every age and station."—*Tablet*.
Treasury of the Sacred Heart. With Epistles and Gospels. 18mo. cloth, 3s. 6d.; roan, 4s. 6d.
Little Treasury of Sacred Heart. 32mo. 2s., roan 2s. 6d.
Manual of Devotion to the Sacred Heart, from the Writings of Bl. Margaret Mary Alacoque. By Denys Casassayas. Translated. 3d.
Act of Consecration to the Sacred Heart. 1d.
Act of Reparation to the Sacred Heart. 1s. per 100.
The Little Prayer-Book for Ordinary Catholic Devotions. Cloth, 3d.
Garden of the Soul, in large type. Roan, gilt edges, 2s.; French morocco, 3s., clasp and rims, 4s. 6d.; French morocco, antique, 3s. 6d.; calf, 5s.; morocco, 6s. 6d.; roan, sprinkled edges, with Epistles and Gospels, 2s. All the other styles with Epistles and Gospels, 6d. extra.
Missal (complete). Persian calf, 8s. 6d.; morocco, 10s. 6d., with rims, 13s. 6d.; morocco, extra gilt, 12s. 6d., with rims, 15s. 6d.; morocco, with turnover edges, 13s. 6d.; morocco antique, 15s.; russia antique, 20s.; ivory, with rims, 31s. 6d.
Catholic Hours: a Manual of Prayer, including Mass and Vespers. By J. R. Digby Beste, Esq. 32mo. cloth, 2s; red edges, 2s. 6d.; roan, 3s.; morocco, 6s.

A Prayer to be said for three days before Holy Communion, and another for three days after. 1d. each, or 6s. 100.
S. Patrick's Manual. By the Poor Clares. 4s. .6d.
Manual of Catholic Piety. Edition with green border.
 * French mor., 2s. 6d. ; mor., 4s.
Occasional Prayers for Festivals. By Rev. T. Barge. 32mo. 4d. and 6d. ; gilt, 1s.
Illustrated Manual of Prayers. 32mo. 3d. ; cloth, 4d.'
Key of Heaven. Very large type, 1s. Leather 2s. 6d. gilt, 3s.
Catholic Piety. 32mo. 6d. ; roan, 1s. ; with Epistles and Gospels, roan, 1s. ; French morocco, 1s. 6d., with rims and clasp, 2s.; imitation ivory, rims and clasp, 2s. 6d. ; velvet rims and clasps, 3s. 6d.
Key of Heaven. Same size and prices.
Catholic Piety, or Key of Heaven, with Epistles and Gospels. Large 32mo. roan 2s. ; French morroco, with rims, 3s. ; extra gilt, 3s. ; with rims, 3s. 6d.
Novena of Meditations in Honour of S. Joseph, according to the method of S. Ignatius; preceded by a new exercise for hearing Mass according to the intentions of the souls in Purgatory. 18mo. 1s. 6d.
Novena to St. Joseph. Translated by M. A. Macdaniel. To which is added a Pastoral of the late Right Rev. Dr. Grant. 32mo. 4d. ; cloth, 6d.
" "All seasons are fitting in which to make Novenas to St. Joseph, for which reason this little work will be found very serviceable at any time."—*Weekly Register.*
A New Year's Gift to our Heavenly Father. 4d.
Devotions for Mass. Very large type, 2d.
Memorare Mass. By the Poor Clares of Kenmare, 2d.
Fourteen Stations of the Holy Way of the Cross. By St. Liguori. Large type edition, 1d.
A Union of our life with the Passion of our Lord by a daily offering. 1s. per 100.
Prayer for one's Confessor. 1s. per 100.
Litany of Resignation. 1s. per 100.

R. Washbourne, 18 *Paternoster Row, London.*

Intentions for Indulgences. 6d. per 100.
Devotions to St. Joseph. 1s. per 100.
Litany of S. Joseph, &c. 1s. per 100.
Devotion to St. Joseph as Patron of the Church. 1d.
Catholic Psalmist: or, Manual of Sacred Music, with the Gregorian Chants for High Mass, Holy Week, &c. Compiled by C. B. Lyons, 4s.
The Complete Hymn Book, 136 Hymns. Price 1d.
Douai Bible. 2s. 6d.; calf or morocco, 6s.; gilt, 7s.
Church Hymns. By J. R. Digby Beste, Esq. 6d.
Catholic Choir Manual: containing Vespers for all the Sundays and Festivals of the year, Hymns and Litanies, &c. Compiled by C. B. Lyons. 1s.
Prayers for the Dying. 1s. per 100.
Indulgenced Prayers for Souls in Purgatory. 1s. per 100.
Indulgenced Prayers for the Rosary of the Holy Souls. 1d. each, 6d. a dozen, 3s. per 100.
The Rosary for the Souls in Purgatory, *with Indulgenced Prayer*. 6d., 8d. and 9d. each. Medals separately, 1d. each, 9s. gross.

Rome, &c.

Two Years in the Pontifical Zouaves. By Joseph Powell, Z.P. With 4 Engravings by Sergeant Collingridge, Z.P. 8vo. 3s. 6d.

"It affords us much pleasure, and deserves the notice of the Catholic public."—*Tablet*. "Familiar names meet the eye on every page, and as few Catholic circles in either country have not had a friend or relative at one time or another serving in the Pontifical Zouaves, the history of the formation of the corps, of the gallant youths, their sufferings, and their troubles, will be valued as something more than a contribution to modern Roman history."—*Freeman's Journal*.

The Victories of Rome. By the Rev. Fr. Kenelm Digby Beste. Second edition. 1s.
Civilization and the See of Rome. By Lord Robert Montague. 6d.
Defence of the Roman Church against Fr. Gratry. By Dom Gueranger. 6d.
Personal Recollections of Rome. By W. J. Jacob, Esq., late of the Pontifical Zouaves. 8vo. 1s. 6d.

The Roman Question. By F. C. Husenbeth, D.D. 1s.
Henri V. (Comte de Chambord), September 29, 1873.
By W. H. Walsh. With a Portrait. 8vo. 1s. 6d.
The Rule of the Pope-King. By Rev. Fr. Martin. 6d.
The Years of Peter. By an Ex-Papal Zouave. 1d.
The Catechism of the Council. By a D.C.L. 2d.

Tales, or Books for the Library.

Tom's Crucifix, and other Tales. By M. F. S. 3s.
"Eight simple stories for the use of teachers of Christian doctrine."—*Universe.* "This is a volume of short, plain, and simple stories, written with the view of illustrating the Catholic religion practically by putting Catholic practices in an interesting light before the mental eyes of children.... The whole of the tales in the volume before us are exceedingly well written."—*Register.*

Simple Tales. Square 16mo. cloth antique, 2s. 6d.
"Contains five pretty stories of a true Catholic tone, interspersed with some short pieces of poetry. . . Are very affecting, and told in such a way as to engage the attention of any child."—*Register.* "This is a little book which we can recommend with great confidence as a present for young readers. The tales are simple, beautiful, and pathetic."—*Catholic Opinion.* "It belongs to a class of books of which the want is generally much felt by Catholic parents."—*Dublin Review.* "Beautifully written. 'Little Terence' is a gem of a Tale."—*Tablet.*

Terry O'Flinn's Examination of Conscience. By the Very Rev. Dr. Tandy. Fcap. 8vo. 1s. 6d. ; extra gilt, 2s. ; cheap edition, 1s.
"The writer possesses considerable literary power."—*Register.* "The idea is well sustained throughout, and when the reader comes to the end of the book he finds the mystery solved, and that it was all nothing but a 'dhrame.'"—*Church Times.*

The Adventures of a Protestant in Search of a Religion : being the Story of a late Student of Divinity at Bunyan Baptist College ; a Nonconformist Minister, who seceded to the Catholic Church. By Iota. 5s. ; cheap edition, 3s.
"Will well repay its perusal."—*Universe.* "This precious volume."—*Baptist.* "No one will deny 'Iota' the merit of entire originality."—*Civilian.* "A valuable addition to every Catholic library." *Tablet.* "There is much cleverness in it."—*Nonconformist.* "Malicious and wicked."—*English Independent.*

A Wasted Life. By Rosa Baughan. 8vo. 3s. 6d.

The Village Lily. Fcap. 8vo. 1s.; gilt, 1s. 6d.

Fairy Tales for Little Children. By Madeleine Howley Meehan. Fcap. 1s.; cloth extra, 1s. 6d.; gilt, 2s.

"Full of imagination and dreams, and at the same time with excellent point and practical aim, within the reach of the intelligence of infants."—*Universe*. "Pleasing, simple stories, combining instruction with amusement."—*Register*.

Rosalie; or, the Memoirs of a French Child. Written by herself. Fcap. 8vo., 1s. and 1s. 6d.; extra gilt, 2s.

"It is prettily told, and in a natural manner. The account of Rosalie's illness and First Communion is very well related. We can recommend the book for the reading of children."—*Tablet*. "The tenth chapter is beautiful."—*Universe*.

The Story of Marie and other Tales. Fcap. 8vo., 2s.; cloth extra, 2s. 6d.; gilt, 3s.; or separately:—The Story of Marie, 2d.; Nelly Blane, and A Contrast, 2d.; A Conversion and a Death-Bed, 2d.; Herbert Montagu, 2d.; Jane Murphy, The Dying Gipsy, and The Nameless Grave, 2d.; The Beggars, and True and False Riches, 2d.; Pat and his Friend, 2d.

"A very nice little collection of stories, thoroughly Catholic in their teaching."—*Tablet*. "A series of short pretty stories, told with much simplicity."—*Universe*. "A number of short pretty stories, replete with religious teaching, told in simple language."—*Weekly Register*.

The Last of the Catholic O'Malleys. A Tale. By M. Taunton. 18mo. cloth, 1s. 6d.; extra, 2s.

"A sad and stirring tale, simply written, and sure to secure for itself readers."—*Tablet*. "Deeply interesting. It is well adapted for parochial and school libraries."—*Weekly Register*. "A very pleasing tale."—*The Month*.

Eagle and Dove. From the French of Mademoiselle Zénaïde Fleuriot. By Emily Bowles. Cr. 8vo., 5s.

"We recommend our readers to peruse this well-written story."—*Register*. "One of the very best stories we have ever dipped into."—*Church Times*. "Admirable in tone and purpose."—*Church Herald*. "A real gain. It possesses merits far above the pretty fictions got up by English writers."—*Dublin Review*. "There is an air of truth and sobriety about this little volume, nor is there any attempt at sensation."—*Tablet*.

Cistercian Legends of the 13th Century. Translated from the Latin by the Rev. Henry Collins. 3s.

Cloister Legends: or, Convents and Monasteries in the Olden Time. *Second Edition.* Cr. 8vo. 4s.

The People's Martyr, a Legend of Canterbury. 4s.

R. Washbourne, 18 Paternoster Row, London.

Rupert Aubray. By the Rev. T. J. Potter. 3s.
Farleyes of Farleye. By the same author. 2s. 6d.
Sir Humphrey's Trial. By the same author. 2s. 6d.
Chats about the Rosary; or, Aunt Margaret's Little Neighbours. Fcap. 8vo. 3s.

"There is scarcely any devotion so calculated as the Rosary to keep up a taste for piety in little children, and we must be grateful for any help in applying its lessons to the daily life of those who already love it in their unconscious tribute to its value and beauty."—*Month.* "We do not know of a better book for reading aloud to children, it will teach them to understand and to love the Rosary."—*Tablet.* "A graceful little book, in fifteen chapters, on the Rosary, illustrative of each of the mysteries, and connecting each with the practice of some particular virtue."—*Catholic Opinion.*

Margarethe Verflassen. Translated from the German by Mrs. Smith Sligo. Fcap. 8vo. 3s.; gilt, 3s. 6d.

"A portrait of a very holy and noble soul, whose life was passed in constant practical acts of the love of God."—*Weekly Register.* "It is the picture of a true woman's life, well fitted up with the practice of ascetic devotion and loving unwearied activity about all the works of mercy."—*Tablet.*

Keighley Hall and other Tales. By Elizabeth King. 18mo. 6d.; cloth, 1s.; gilt, 1s. 6d.; or, separately, Keighley Hall, Clouds and Sunshine, The Maltese Cross, 3d. each.
Sir Ælfric and other Tales. By the Rev. G. Bampfield. 18mo. 6d.; cloth, 1s.; gilt, 1s. 6d.
Ned Rusheen. By the Poor Clares. Crown 8vo. 6s.
The Prussian Spy. A Novel. By V. Valmont. 4s.
Adolphus; or, the Good Son. 18mo. gilt, 6d.
Nicholas; or, the Reward of a Good Action. 6d.
The Lost Children of Mount St. Bernard. 18mo. gilt, 6d.
The Baker's Boy; or, the Results of Industry. 6d.

"All prettily got up, artistically illustrated, and pleasantly-written. Better books for gifts and rewards we do not know."—*Weekly Register.* "We can thoroughly recommend them."—*Tablet.*

The Truce of God: a Tale of the Eleventh Century. By G. H. Miles. 4s.
Tales and Sketches. By Charles Fleet. 8vo. cloth, 2s. and 2s. 6d.; cloth, gilt, 3s. 6d.

"Pleasingly-written, and containing some valuable hints. There is a good deal of nice feeling in these short stories."—*Tablet.*

A Broken Chain. 18mo. gilt, 6d.
The Convent Prize Book. By the author of "Geraldine." Fcap. 8vo. 2s. 6d.; gilt, 3s. 6d.
The Journey of Sophia and Eulalie to the Palace of True Happiness. Translated by the Rev. Father Ambrose, Mount St. Bernard's. Fcap. 8vo. 3s. 6d.; cheap edition, 2s. 6d.
The Fisherman's Daughter. By Conscience. 4s.
The Amulet. By Hendrick Conscience. 4s.
Count Hugo of Graenhove. By Conscience. 4s.
The Village Innkeeper. By Conscience. 4s.
Happiness of being Rich. By Conscience. 4s.
Florence O'Neill. By A. M. Stewart. 4s. 6d. and 6s.
Limerick Veteran. By the same. 4s. 6d. and 6s.
The Three Elizabeths. By the same. 3s. 6d. and 4s. 6d.
Alone in the World. By the same. 3s. 6d. and 4s. 6d.
Festival Tales. By J. F. Waller. 5s.
Shakespeare's Plays and Tragedies. Abridged and Revised for the use of Schools. By Rosa Baughan. 8vo. 7s. 6d.
Poems. By H. N. Oxenham. *Third Edition.* 3s. 6d.

Miscellaneous and Educational.

History of Modern Europe. With a Preface by the Right Rev. Dr. Weathers. 12mo. cloth, 5s.; gilt, 6s.; roan, 5s. 6d.

"A work of special importance for the way in which it deals with the early part of the present Pontificate."—*Weekly Register.*

The Continental Fish Cook; or, a Few Hints on Maigre Dinners. By M. J. N. de Frederic. 18mo. 1s.

"This is an admirable collection of recipes, which many housekeepers will welcome for use. We strongly recommend our lady readers at once to procure it."—*Church Herald.* "It will give to all mistresses of households very valuable hints on maigre dinners, and we feel sure they will be glad to know of the existence of such a manual."—*Register.* "There are 103 recipes, all of which have been practically tested; they combine variety, wholesomeness, and economy."—*Universe.* "It is an unpretending little work, but nevertheless containing many recipes, enabling housekeepers to provide an excellent variety of dishes, such as may lawfully be eaten in times of fasting and abstinence."—*Church Times.*

R. Washbourne, 18 Paternoster Row, London.

Culpepper. An entirely New Edition of Brook's Family Herbal. 150 engravings, drawn and coloured from living specimens. Crown 8vo., 5s. 6d.

University Education, under the Guidance of the Church ; or, Monastic Studies. By a Monk of St. Augustine's, Ramsgate. 8vo. 2s. 6d.

"An admirable pamphlet. Its contents are above praise. We trust that it will be widely circulated."—*Weekly Register.* "The author is evidently a scholar, a well-read man, and a person of experience and wide reading. His essay, consequently, is worth both studying and preserving."—*Church Herald.*

Elements of Philosophy, comprising Logic, and General Principles of Metaphysics. By Rev. W. H. Hill, S.J. Second edition, 8vo. 6s.

"This work is from the pen of one who has devoted many years to the study and teaching of philosophy. It is elementary, and must be concise; yet it treats the important points of philosophy so clearly, and contains so many principles of wide application, that it cannot fail to be especially useful in a country where sound philosophical doctrine is perhaps more needed than in any other."

History of England. By W. Mylius. 12mo. 3s. 6d.

Catechism of the History of England. Cloth, 1s.

History of Ireland. By T. Young. 18mo. cloth, 2s. 6d.

The Illustrated History of Ireland. By the Nun of Kenmare. Illustrated by Doyle. 8vo. 11s.

The Patriots' History of Ireland. By the Poor Clares of Kenmare. 18mo. cloth, 2s. ; cloth gilt, 2s. 6d.

A Chronological Sketch of the Kings of England and France. With Anecdotes for the use of Children. By H. Murray Lane. 2s. 6d. ; or separately, England, 1s. 6d., France, 1s. 6d.

"Admirably adapted for teaching young children the elements of English and French history."—*Tablet.* "A very useful little publication."—*Weekly Register.* "An admirably arranged little work for the use of children."—*Universe.*

The Catholic Alphabet of Scripture Subjects. Price, on a sheet, plain, 1s. ; coloured, 2s. ; mounted on linen, to fold in a case, 3s. 6d. ; varnished, on linen, on rollers, 4s.

"This will be hailed with joy by all young children in Catholic schools, and we should gladly see it placed conspicuously before the eyes of our little ones."—*Catholic Opinion.* "Will be very welcome in the infant school."—*Weekly Register.*

Bell's Modern Reader and Speaker. Cloth, 3s. 6d.
General Questions in History, Chronology, Geography, the Arts, &c. By A. M. Stewart. 4s. 6d.
Extracts from the Fathers and other Writers of the Church. 12mo. cloth, 4s. 6d.
Brickley's Standard Table Book, ½d.
Washbourne's Multiplication Table on a sheet, 3s. per 100. Specimen sent for 1d. stamp.

Music (*Net*).

BY HERR WILHELM SCHULTHES.

Veni Domine. Motett for Four Voices. 2s. ; vocal arrangement, 6d.
Cor Jesu, Salus in Te Sperantium. 2s.; with harp accompaniment, 2s. 6d. ; abridged edition, 3d.
Mass of the Holy Child Jesus, and Ave Maria for unison and congregational singing, with organ accompaniment. 3s.
The Vocal Part. 4d. ; or in cloth, 6d.
The Ave Maria of this Mass can be had for Four Voices, with the Ingressus Angelus. 1s. 3d.
Recordare. Oratio Jeremiæ Prophetæ. 1s.
Ne projicias me a facie Tua. Motett for Four Voices. (T.B.) 1s. 3d.
Benediction Service, with 36 Litanies. 6s.
Oratory Hymns. 2 vols., 8s.
Regina Cœli. Motett for Four Voices. 3s. ; vocal arrangement, 1s.
Twelve Latin Hymns, for Vespers, &c. 2s.

Litanies. By Rev. J. McCarthy. 1s. 3d.
Six Litany Chants. By F. Leslie. 6d.
Ave Maria. By T. Haydn Waud. 1s. 6d.
Fr. Faber's Hymns. Various, 9d. each.
Portfolio. With a patent metallic back. 3s.

A separate Catalogue of FOREIGN Books, Educational Books, Books for the Library or for Prizes, supplied ; also a Catalogue of School and General Stationery, a Catalogue of Secondhand Books, and a Catalogue of Crucifixes and other Religious Articles.

INDEX TO AUTHORS.

	PAGE		PAGE
A'Kempis, Thomas	8	King, Miss	28
Allies, T. W., Esq.	11	Lacordaire, Père	12
Amherst, Bishop	8	Laing, Rev. Dr.	13, 16, 21
Bagshawe, Rev. Fr.	22	Lane, H. Murray, Esq.	30
Bagshawe, Rev. J. B.	14, 15	Lockhart, Rev. Fr.	13
Bampfield, Rev. G.	28	M'Corry, Rev. Dr.	17
Barge, Rev. T.	23	Macdaniel, Miss	21, 24
Beste, J. R. D., Esq.	10, 23, 25	Macleod, Rev. X. D.	21
Beste, Rev. K. D.	25	Manning, Most Rev. Dr.	13, 19
Bethell, Rev. A. P.	21	Marshall, T. W. M., Esq.	10
Blosius	7	Meehan, Madeleine Howley	26
Boudon, Mgr.	7	Milner, Bishop	23
Bowles, Emily	27	Nary, Rev. J.	15
Bradbury, Rev. Fr.	29	Nevin, Willis	2
Bridges, Miss	1	Newman, Dr.	19
Brownlow, Rev. W. R. B.	5, 13	Oratorian Lives of the Saints	18
Burder, Rt. Rev. Abbot	6	Oxenham, H. N.	11, 29
Burke, S. H., M.A.	12	Ozanam, Professor	2
Butler, Alban	8, 17	Passionist Fathers	13
Challoner, Bishop	16	Philpin, Rev. Fr.	6
Collins, Rev. Fr.	9	Poirier, Bishop	16
Conscience, Hendrick	29	Poor Clares of Kenmare	12, 20
Darras, Abbé	7	Powell, J., Esq.	25
Deham, Rev. A.	23	Pye, H. J., Esq.	16
Dupanloup, Mgr.	2	Ravignan, Père	8
Fleuriot, Mdlle. Zénaïde	27	Redmond, Rev. Dr.	1, 13
Francis of Sales, St.	10, 11	Richardson, Rev. Fr.	17
Frassinetti	14	Robertson, Professor	11, 13
Gibson, Rev. H.	15	Scaramelli	9
Gilmour, Rev. R.	16	Schulthes, Herr	31
Goffine, Rev. Fr.	16	Shakespeare	29
Grace Ramsay	19	Ségur, Mgr. de	17
Grant, Bishop	11, 24	Shepard, T. S., Esq.	19
Gueranger	25	Sligo, A. V. Smith, Esq.	17
Hedley, Canon	7	Sligo, Mrs. Smith	27
Herbert, Lady	1, 2, 6	Stewart, A. M.	29
Hill, Rev. Fr.	30	Tame, C. E., Esq.	21
Hope, Mrs.	9	Tandy, Very Rev. Dr.	26
Husenbeth, Very Rev. Dr.	20, 21	Taunton, Mrs.	27
Kenny, Dr.	17	Williams, Canon	16

CONTENTS.

	PAGE		PAGE
New Books	1	Prayer-Books	22
Dramas, Comedies, Farces	3	Rome, &c.	25
Religious Reading	5	Tales, or Books for Library	26
Religious Instruction	14	Educational Works	29
Lives of Saints, &c.	17	Music	31
Our Lady, Works relating to	20		

R. WASHBOURNE, 18 PATERNOSTER ROW.

www.ingramcontent.com/pod-product-compliance
Lightning Source LLC
Chambersburg PA
CBHW022112230426
43672CB00008B/1352